Praise for *You*
From a

'Mark Shayler is a pioneer of the notion that going green is good for business, and this brilliantly accessible book shows how every workplace can make a difference for the planet and still be a business winner.' HUGH FEARNLEY-WHITTINGSTALL, FOUNDER OF RIVER COTTAGE AND ENVIRONMENTAL CAMPAIGNER

'This is the book I was waiting for. With his characteristic verve and straight-talking swagger, Mark Shayler shows you the sustainability bits that matter and ditches the ones that don't. Suddenly everything makes sense! Keep this book in your back pocket for meetings, project pitches and getting lost in the forest. A must-read and a must-act book that illuminates your path every step of the way.' LUCY SIEGLE, JOURNALIST AND AUTHOR

'All small businesses should read this book because it's a revolution waiting to happen. I truly believe that business can change the world and nobody breaks down the steps to making a profit with principles better than Mark Shayler does here. If you want to make a (real) difference but aren't sure how, this is a superb place to start.' HOLLY TUCKER MBE, FOUNDER OF HOLLY & CO AND NOTONTHEHIGHSTREET, AND UK BUSINESS AMBASSADOR FOR SMALL CREATIVE BUSINESSES

'An honest and enlightening manifesto for change. Between the sober truth and some reasons to be cheerful, Mark Shayler highlights the brutal reality of our current road to terminal illness, while explaining that every business can contribute to our road to recovery by correctly harnessing the power of its people. Energy. Circularity. Mobility. Regeneration. Resilience. Education. Activism. If any of these words are resonant with you, this book is your must-have guide to understanding the impact of doing business on the planet, providing a multitude of options to rethink and reinvent why an accountable, progressive and regenerative business culture is the key to designing a better future.' RAOUL SHAH, FOUNDER AND CEO, THE CASBAH GROUP

'Mark Shayler has been around a bit in the world of corporate sustainability – in fact, for over 30 years. And he's worked with a shedload of companies during that time. So he knows what he's talking about, the anecdotes are authentic, and his humour a tonic in what can be very arid territory. Part how-to primer, part explainer of all things relevant, and part celebration of the power of creative design, *You Can't Make Money from a Dead Planet* ticks all the boxes.' SIR JONATHAN PORRITT, ENVIRONMENTALIST AND FORMER DIRECTOR OF FRIENDS OF THE EARTH

You Can't Make Money From a Dead Planet

*The sustainable method
for driving profits*

Mark Shayler

KoganPage

Publisher's note
Every possible effort has been made to ensure that the information contained in this book is accurate at the time of going to press, and the publishers and author cannot accept responsibility for any errors or omissions, however caused. No responsibility for loss or damage occasioned to any person acting, or refraining from action, as a result of the material in this publication can be accepted by the editor, the publisher or the author.

First published in Great Britain and the United States in 2023 by Kogan Page Limited

2nd Floor, 45 Gee Street
London
EC1V 3RS
United Kingdom

8 W 38th Street, Suite 902
New York, NY 10018
USA

4737/23 Ansari Road
Daryaganj
New Delhi 110002
India

www.koganpage.com

Kogan Page books are printed on paper from sustainable forests.

ISBNs
Hardback   978 1 3986 1204 4
Paperback   978 1 3986 1202 0
Ebook   978 1 3986 1203 7

British Library Cataloguing-in-Publication Data
A CIP record for this book is available from the British Library.

Library of Congress Cataloging-in-Publication Data
Names: Shayler, Mark, author.
Title: You can't make money from a dead planet : the sustainable method for driving profits / Mark Shayler.
Description: London ; New York, NY : KoganPage, 2023. | Includes bibliographical references and index.
Identifiers: LCCN 2023031535 (print) | LCCN 2023031536 (ebook) | ISBN 9781398612044 (hardback) | ISBN 9781398612020 (paperback) | ISBN 9781398612037 (ebook)
Subjects: LCSH: Business–Environmental aspects. | Profit–Environmental aspects. | Sustainable development.
Classification: LCC HD30.255 .S466 2023 (print) | LCC HD30.255 (ebook) | DDC 658.4/08–dc23/eng/20230725
LC record available at https://lccn.loc.gov/2023031535
LC ebook record available at https://lccn.loc.gov/2023031536

Typeset by Integra Software Services, Pondicherry
Print production managed by Jellyfish
Printed and bound by CPI Group (UK) Ltd, Croydon, CR0 4YY

This book is dedicated to my adult kids (Daisy, Max, Tilly and Mabel) and my grandkids (Juni and the ones yet to be born). We need to hand over a better world than the one we have created; better politically, socially and environmentally. We need to pass on a beacon of hope. Because there is still hope: hope and community; hope and kindness; hope and joy.
What is not transformed is transferred.

Contents

Acknowledgements viii

Introduction 1

1 Where are we and how did we get here? 6
2 You can't make money from a dead planet 11
3 The main environmental challenges 19
4 Business impacts 37
5 Is there any good news? 68
6 How do we do good and still turn a profit? 104
7 The strategic tools you need to change your business 126
8 The practical and science-based tools to change your business (and still make a profit) 155
9 Re-framing business 210
10 The regenerative business 220

'The last chapter' 256

Notes 268
Index 279

For further resources, including tables, templates and a bonus chapter, visit www.markshayler.com/deadplanet

Acknowledgements

People help you as you go through life. Most people are nice, most people will help you and sometimes they do so without realising it. Sometimes it can just be a word of encouragement, other times something significantly bigger. So here is a list of thanks for those that have helped me, some of them may not know it:

Nicola Shayler, Daisy Shayler, Max Shayler, Tilly Shayler, Mabel Shayler, My parents, Tom Dolman, Guy Shayler, Gareth Bruff, Miles Allkins, Dai Larner, Jeff Spencer, Amanda Dalton, Waqar Siraj, Mark Fisher, John Dutton, Colin Savage, John Roberts, Mrs Jackson, David Willets, John Wilkinson (geography matters), Charlie Gladstone, Sue Norman, The Purple Y-Fronts, Mrs Thomas, Johnathon Porritt, Sophie Thomas, Pam Warhurst, The BOBs, the MKP, George Abramson, everyone at Kogan Page, Chris Cudmore.

An additional shout-out to our son Max who works with me and does all the carbon work we deliver. He helped to simplify the carbon foot printing methodology in this book and is way better at that stuff than I ever was.

Introduction

As I walked through the main hall at The United Nations Climate Change Conference, COP26 in Glasgow in November 2021, I stopped to observe people taking selfies against the backdrop of the large suspended globe. I tried to imagine the LinkedIn and Instagram captions:

'Here I am at COP26, you gotta do your bit right?'
'Take a good look, it's the only planet we've got.'
'At ACME we are committed to selling the shit we make and that nobody wants in a sustainable way.'

Now of course no-one actually typed the last of these but there were hundreds of the first two. There was a feeling of 'green cocking' about the whole thing. This phrase is a portmanteau created by a good friend, lecturer and circular designer Claire Potter. Greenwashing mixed with peacocking.

It perfectly describes where we were at the time of COP26. It doesn't describe where we are now though. I would use the phrase 'green ducking' now. What I mean by this is the hiding of corporate environmental commitments. This happens for two reasons: first the fear of scrutiny, and second the fear of criticism for trying to do the right thing. The focus on greenwashing by regulators and the public will result in businesses hiding their environmentally positive activities in case they attract broader criticism. More on this later.

I've worked in sustainability since 1990. To be more precise I've worked in business sustainability since 1990. This is a tough place to work and it has changed massively (more on this in Chapter 1). Whilst it is clear that our past and current models of business have created the vast majority of the world's problems; I believe that enterprise is the only thing that can solve them. Before I get a load of flak for that allow me to explain myself.

The problem with capitalism

There is something fundamentally broken at the heart of capitalism and that is its inability to place value on things that have been, historically, cheap or free. At its core capitalism is an economic system based on the private ownership of the means of production (raw materials, labour and manufacturing capacity) and their operation for profit. This is flawed in many ways. Labour is people. The idea of owning people is utterly redundant. Labour used to be seen as heads and bodies, and increasingly it's brains. Labour is not owned; that gives the perception of it being static when it has never been more fluid. It gives the impression of labour being faceless, a unit working for nothing more than financial reward, when it has never been less so. We will get on to the chasing of cheap labour around the world later.

The idea of labour being owned is at odds with social progression. Recent research by Edelman[1] indicates that not only is the consumer increasingly belief driven but so too is the employee. This research identified that, in terms of employee must-haves, social and environmental concerns are approaching equivalence with salary. Edelman have been benchmarking employee perceptions over the last decade and the most recent published in 2022 identifies that in terms of reasons to join or stay with a business, social impact sits at 71 per cent (up five points in the three years since 2018). Career advancement is at 82 per cent and personal empowerment at 77 per cent. The gap is closing. To be fair it is wrong to see this as a gap but rather a complex web of reasons to stay somewhere or join somewhere. We can maybe translate this complexity as trust. More than three-quarters of respondents said they have higher expectations of employers than three years ago. It would (maybe) be easy to see this as an issue for the middle-class employee, something to consider only once basic needs have been met. But the research indicates otherwise. Edelman identified especially high numbers in developing markets (India – 88 per cent; Brazil – 81 per cent).

This is fascinating and a litmus test for our perceptions of business, values and self-worth. Of particular interest is the 61 per cent of respondents who stated they choose their employer based on beliefs, including refusal to work at the company because of disagreement on social issues. This question had a particularly high response (87 per cent) in China. I will return to this research later.

Now, I know what you're thinking: *Shayler slipped-in the word 'Consumer' earlier and surely that's part of the problem?* Yes it is, and it's a word that I don't like to use. I prefer customer (actually, I prefer citizen) but the business world has lots of B2B (business-to-business) customers that make up the 'value chain' (this is a progression of activities that businesses perform in order to deliver a valuable product, and yes, it's a horrible phrase. I dislike most business language and am on a mission to remove such drivel as 'day partings' (meals), 'going forwards' (a pointless addition to sentences to make the speaker look progressive), 'robust' (be specific, do you mean economically beneficial, an aggressive challenge, really?). The value chain is simply the supply chain with added emphasis on who adds value (profit) to the final product. Therefore, for simplicity and to avoid uncertainty I will use consumer to mean the end customer.

But clearly seeing people as units of consumption who graze through products and services, getting rid of waste as they go, is a little unhelpful to say the least. We will return to this theme later.

So if employees want to work for better businesses, if the public are demanding products with less impact and if the world is on a knife edge in terms of ecological system collapse why hasn't business changed?

Well, it has. But not enough and not fast enough.

This book will explain how we got here, how we can do better, how we can still make a profit and protect people and planet, and how you can start. The aim is to help you develop a business and a team that are aligned with social and environmental good, and still make a profit. Profit isn't bad – it's what we do with it that matters.

The book is divided into 10 chapters (along with an Introduction and Conclusion) and is intended to be read through from the beginning to the end. But there are accompanying worksheets and tools available on www.noplanet noprofit.com that will allow you to start on this journey and turn your business around, which will allow you stay relevant and profitable while doing less harm.

I begin by setting out the context and how we got into the position we are in; I then outline the main environmental challenges that we face and move on to how this is impacted by business and vice versa; I then look at the good news that is hiding between the problems before moving onto what business can do about it.

CHAPTER ONE

Where are we and how did we get here?

I'm old. At the time of writing I'm 54. I went to university a year late as I messed up my A Levels. This was a blessing in disguise. Rather than heading off to Bristol University to study law I had another year to think things through and I opted to study Environmental Science and Geography at Bradford University. I started in 1988. In all honesty choosing a degree was really difficult. As someone who had a scientific approach but was also creative (we are all creative) and loved the humanities I really struggled with what to study. So I chose all the subjects. Some science, some humanity and some art. The beauty of the degree I studied was that I could understand the science behind sustainability, look at how it impacted and was impacted by people and then design solutions to these problems. The separation of these issues – science, art and humanity is at the centre of our environmental crisis. The singular pursuit of profit at all costs created a system of extraction and exploitation that has taken centuries to disassemble.

Marx summed it up with his equation:

Raw Materials + Labour = Product + Profit + Waste

The problem here is that three of the elements of this equation were undervalued, massively.

Raw materials were taken from nature at little or no cost. Labour was alarmingly cheap in the West and when considered too expensive was bolstered by slavery. Once this was outlawed labour drifted eastwards to lower income countries. Less exploitative than slavery but still exploitative. Manufacturing began drifting eastwards from the 1970s in search of lower labour costs and un-unionized workforces. A secondary 'benefit' of this drift of manufacturing to the East was more relaxed (or non-existent) environmental regulations. Operating in a low-regulation country or province initially reduces costs but ultimately it's like peeing in your own bath water. It won't do you any good in the long run.

There are many lessons from history here. The one closest to my heart is the story of Titus Salt. Salt was a Wool Baron in Bradford. The city used to be the centre of British wool textiles. It was a low-wage economy surrounded by great grazing land and a large supply of cheap labour. Twinned with industrial advancement Bradford saw a boom in its fortunes in the 1840s and 50s as between 80 and 90 per cent of the wool sold around the world had its origins in the city. This combination of cheap labour, good quality and low-priced raw materials, and then a technological innovation, saw the growth of wool scouring (cleaning the wool), washing and dying. This in turn created a high level of water pollution that made the workforce who drank it ill and polluted the water coming into the process.

Back to Titus. He saw this happening and to preserve the workforce and the quality of the product he knew he needed to move his factory out of the city. He chose a greenfield site some 7 km from the city and designed and built a factory (Salts Mill) and a village for his workforce. He did this on the bank of the River Aire so he had both water power and fresh water, and importantly it was above the smoke line of the city, thereby avoiding deaths and illness from air pollution.

Other companies followed suit for the same reasons. The city is the home to the modern Labour movement and the workforce quickly became unionized, demanding higher wages and better conditions. This increased the cost of labour, and in the 1970s the city experienced an immigration boom as skilled textile workers from Pakistan arrived to work in the industry. Tighter environmental requirements and the unionization of the newly arrived workers meant that manufacturers chased cheaper labour and lower environmental requirements (this usually means cheaper product manufacture) around the world. The customer got cheaper items, but profits were still high – the planet and the workers paid the price. China and India became the centres of textiles manufacture, and now we are hooked on fast fashion at the expense of people and planet.

We are seeing this play out further afield as the manufacturing centres of China impose tighter environmental regulations. Furthermore, as wages rise, manufacturing moves further inland and ultimately to Africa. China's investment in Africa is astonishing. China's FDI stock in Africa totalled $110 billion in 2019 contributing over 20 per cent to Africa's growth[1] and a third of Africa's power grid and energy infrastructure is financed by Chinese state-owned companies.

This investment is a new form of colonialism and is paving the way for the re-imagination of the African continent as a low-wage manufacturing centre. With this comes all the risks of the last wave of colonialism, and we know how that ended. The potential of Africa as an economic power and an environmental power is unparalleled. It's worth pausing here to reflect upon this.

The control of resources is the control of economy. If you don't have access to raw materials then you can't make things, if you can't make them then you can't sell them, if you can't sell them then you can't make money.

We will dig into the need to transition away from the linear economy (take-make-use-dispose) later but the current version of capitalism is still propped up on under-valued labour, resources and environmental sinks (environmental sinks are the absorption of human-made waste by the environment). Back when I was studying environmental science at university, one of our lecturers had a mantra: 'dilution is the solution to pollution'. The thing is that it wasn't and isn't. That's the kind of thinking that got us into this mess.

Traditionally, in order to grow economically we needed to convert raw materials into products and products into economic capital and then ensure that there is a continuing growth in desire for these products. Aligning consumerism with happiness and success was the masterstroke here and it fuelled an advertising industry that thrived on telling lies (more on this later).

But, I hear you ask, isn't consumption good for the economy?

CHAPTER TWO

You can't make money from a dead planet

There is no economy on a dead planet, and the key challenge that we have is how we make more money by selling and consuming less 'stuff'. This will become the focal point of the next 50 years of civilization and, in my opinion, is the greatest opportunity we have in terms of innovation. Placing sustainability at the heart of the innovation process rather than at the end means that it becomes an accelerator rather than a brake on creativity.

The link between economy and ecology is always with us. Our primary sources of heat and food, wealth and power, are all extracted from nature. The word 'eco' comes from the Greek word Oikos meaning family, home and property.

Ecology is the study of the house and relationships in it. It is the study of relationships between living organisms.

Economics means the management of Oikos, of our home. It doesn't mean the merciless extraction of value from nature in a way that leaves nature struggling to recover.

How did they get placed in opposition to each other? The problem began when value was stripped from nature faster than it could be re-built. This is what unsustainable means. Taking a natural resource and using it at a faster rate than it can be re-built. Or emitting gases or wastes faster than they can be re-absorbed by nature or society. We passed this point over a century ago. In essence we have been building an economy for today based on the resources of tomorrow, running our account into the red.

This started with the industrial revolution but seriously hit its stride after the Second World War. Post-war, the way to grow economically, to create jobs, to create wealth, was to build a consumer economy. Mass production creates jobs but needs mass consumption, and for mass consumption we really need mass dissatisfaction. Not political dissatisfaction but dissatisfaction with self-worth and social standing. This drives consumption as a route to joy.

This was spotted as a problem early on by author, journalist and social critic Vance Packard in his 1960 book *The Waste Makers*. The core premise of the book is American society over-emphasizes consumption, particularly quantity over quality. In so doing it sacrifices environmental protection, culture, health and a proper concern for the future.

Planned obsolescence

In *The Waste Makers* Vance Packard introduces the reader to the concepts of planned obsolescence and disposability. We will build on these themes later but it is clear that the more we consume, the more waste we produce, the more carbon we emit and the more resources we burn through. The secret to planned obsolescence is giving the consumer enough satisfaction that they don't feel cheated but not enough durability that they keep the product for too long. Short product lifespans are great for profit, but bad for the planet. The nirvana is building products and services that are great for both.

So how does planned obsolescence work?

1 Functional obsolescence

It was, and is, not uncommon for manufacturers to include a component that wore out faster than the rest of the product. This tended to be electric motors in white goods or domestic goods, given the price of repairing or replacing these items is very close to buying a new product. This was a common practice in product design and manufacture in the 1950s and still happens today. Some drills, for example, are designed for a maximum of 60 minutes of drilling before the motors burn out. A motor that lasts five times as long only costs 20 per cent more. Corporations are in a continual battle to tweak their business model to ensure customer satisfaction and loyalty and make sure that their products don't last so long that they cut off their income streams.

In addition to individual companies designing products with shortened lives there are also examples of companies working together to agree to shorten the lives of products across the sector. The most famous example of this was the coming together of the light bulb industry in 1924 to form the Phoebus cartel. This cartel was formed for two main reasons. The first was to divide business between territories with non-compete arrangements. The second and most relevant reason was to agree to a shortening of the life of the incandescent light bulb. The cartel agreed to shorten the life from 2,500 hours to 1,000 hours and therefore increased both their profit and the waste generated.

Switching sectors to fashion, the thing that currently gets me frustrated is the use of plastic heels on shoes rather than rubber ones. They wear through in a matter of days; sure they can be replaced with longer-lasting rubber heels but the cost of using rubber in the first place would be pennies (or cents) more, not pounds (or dollars). Fast fashion is famous for low-quality, short-life products. *The New York Times* reported that the average fast fashion garment is constructed to last for 10 wears.[1] This isn't about things going out of fashion, this is about the items being made so badly that they wear out.

I have a personal example here. Back in the late 1980s I bought a grey t-shirt from the newly launched Next Directory. It was great. Roll on 10 years and I thought I'd buy another, so I went to the store and bought what looked like the same t-shirt, for about the same price (no inflation in 10 years?). It lasted one year. The seams twisted, it bobbled and it looked rubbish. In fact, my original one was still going long after the new one had fallen apart. What had happened in those intervening 10 years?

Well, firstly the company had lost its way. Strategically. They had forgotten who they were for, they had forgotten their 'why'. In my opinion this is arguably still the case. Secondly, the rise of fast fashion had made them believe that they were in a race to the bottom in terms of price. This in turn creates a compromise in terms of the materials used. Cheaper cotton and weaker stitching. I used to work in one of the Next stores in Leicester in 1988–90 and it had a very clear position and purpose. Over 10 years that had been diluted and the company had lost its clear design ethos and quality attributes. We will talk about purpose in great detail later in Chapter 7 but it is no surprise that when a company loses theirs they lose a little bit of the magic that they started with. There is also the issue of losing the founder; this too dilutes purpose and replaces it with other values.

2 Technological obsolescence

This overlaps with functional obsolescence but is less about parts wearing out and more about systems slowing down. As things become controlled by silicon chips and given the galloping rate of development of processing power it's inevitable that product life cycles in some categories will be shortened. This is simply a function of the speed of technological advancement. However, there are more mischievous forces at play here. In February 2020 Apple were fined $27 million for the practice of slowing down older phones.[2] Then in November of the same year they settled a legal case against them by paying $113 million to settle a class action lawsuit. They argued that this was to 'prolong the life of the devices'. They had been doing this since 2017 and it is clear from reading customer feedback that many people had upgraded their phones as a result of a drop in performance. As long ago as the 1950s manufacturers chose to build a weaker component into the product – now they can effectively 'brick' devices (make them slow and effectively redundant) with a software update. Apple are not alone, iFixit (a global community of people helping each other fix things) rated Microsoft products as being worse than Apple in their Repairability Index.

3 Emotional obsolescence

This is the interesting one. Years ago, I used to be Design Counsellor for the UK business support organization Business Link. They in turn were supported by the UK Design Council (an incredible organization championing good design since 1944) and we used one of their tools called Designing Demand. It was great but the name really hit me. As an environmentalist with a role in design I felt that we needed to design demand out, not in. But the advent of emotional design is a great platform for stimulating consumption. If you can design demand, desire, even love for a product or service then you don't need to build in technological or functional obsolescence, you just need to change how people feel about a product. If you can make them feel dissatisfied or even less-in-love with it than they did then you've got a sale.

A great example of this is the folding phone adverts that Samsung launched in 2022. They were beautifully conceived and produced. They spoke directly to emotional obsolescence and our desires. They even made me question my choice of phone (which is actually a choice of operating system and tech ecosystem) and consider one that folds in half. Reader, I resisted.

We see this approach to creating dissatisfaction in the fashion world. The whole industry depends on you falling in, then out, of love with a look, of almost being embarrassed by a piece or at least the way it makes you appear. You can't be seen to be 'behind the times' in this world. It's an entire industry built upon emotional obsolescence; therefore, it's no wonder that a counter-movement has begun. Slow fashion is an antidote to fast fashion and it celebrates the scars and wear patterns that emerge in clothes that we keep for a long time, in clothes that age with us. Raw selvedge denim, for example, is a labour of love to break in. Best to not wash it for six months (this in itself massively reduces the carbon footprint of the first year of wear) and then only once a month. After six months you will be able to see the outline of your wallet/phone, the whiskers behind your knees and wear on the pockets and thighs. Washing at six months reveals these. These are now your jeans, no-one else's. You've created your own emotional attachment to the jeans that enhances them and is likely to extend your ownership. The challenge here is how to make a $200 pair of jeans accessible to all; more on that in Chapter 9 when we discuss business plans.

We have an economy based upon the processing of materials into products that create utility or joy and profit. Our economy is important, money is a powerful tool and profit is not a dirty word. The challenge that we have is how we make more money by selling less stuff, and how we generate more joy by consuming less stuff. We return to these challenges later in the book.

It is clear that the very nature of our economic system, of capitalism, has created many of the social and economic problems. However, this doesn't mean that we need to throw capitalism away or replace it with socialism (tempting as it is). We are in too deep to do this. But we do need to reform capitalism and bring out a more caring version where other social good is valued as highly as money.

Let's dig into the main environmental challenges that we currently face.

CHAPTER THREE

The main environmental challenges

There is much damage that we have inflicted upon the planet. This chapter will give an overview of the main challenges we face and look at the numbers behind them. This is not an exhaustive list and I'm not saying that issues not discussed here are not important.

1 Climate change

Climate change is the large-scale, long-term changing of global or regional climatic patterns owing to anthropogenic emissions of greenhouse gases. Surprisingly, some

70 years after an internal White House memo and over 125 years since a seminal paper by Swedish scientist Svante Arrhenius first predicted that changes in atmospheric carbon dioxide (CO_2) levels could substantially alter the surface temperature through the greenhouse effect, climate change still creates contention. The statistics, as we will soon see, are clear and evidenced, however this has become political and part of the 'fake news' and 'anti-woke' agenda. This bundles it up with a series of theories and attempts to introduce just enough doubt on facts. America is particularly open to this kind of suggestion. In 1938, Guy Callendar connected CO_2 increases in Earth's atmosphere to global warming and there is a hidden White House memo from 1977 acknowledging the possibility of 'catastrophic climate change' due to the release of fossil CO_2.

Let's look at the science.

Climate change has severe negative impacts upon extreme weather patterns, sea levels, food production and harvest security, ocean temperatures and acidity, flooding and prevalence of waterborne diseases.

This is serious stuff.

The evidence for climate change in response to anthropogenic emission of greenhouse gases is irrefutable, with global CO_2 emissions having increased by 400 per cent since the year 1950, resulting in the concentration of atmospheric CO_2 having reached 400 ppm (parts per million).

On 28 November 2022 the average concentration of atmospheric CO_2 was 417.31 ppm. This has increased from 411.27 in two years, and from 389.16 ppm in 2011.

The last time in history that concentrations of atmospheric CO_2 exceeded 400 ppm was roughly four million years ago, during the Pliocene era. During this time, global temperatures were 2–4°C warmer than current, and sea levels were 10–25 meters higher than they currently are.

The rise of global average temperatures mirrors atmospheric CO_2 concentrations. Take a look at the data from NOAA NCEI[1] (they are the United States' leading authority on environmental data, and manage one of the largest archives of atmospheric, coastal, geophysical and oceanic research in the world). Similar data has been published by the IPCC (the Intergovernmental Panel on Climate Change) and the mirroring of global temperatures and atmospheric concentrations of carbon dioxide is as clear as can be.

Furthermore, 9 of the 10 hottest years on record occurred in the last decade, and 2021 was the 45th consecutive year with global temperatures above the 20th century average.

So the world is clearly warming. But how?

The carbon cycle

The carbon cycle is the cycle that continually moves carbon from the atmosphere to the earth and then back again, and again, and again. On the earth, carbon is stored in rocks, sediments, the ocean and living organisms. It is released back into the atmosphere through the burning of fossil fuels, plants and animals dying as well as when fires burn and volcanoes erupt.

The carbon cycle balances the concentration of carbon in the different reservoirs on the planet. These reservoirs try and hold carbon in broad equilibrium, however a change in the amount of carbon in one reservoir affects all the others. Since the industrial revolution the cycle has been disturbed by the burning of fossil fuels, which release large amounts of carbon dioxide into the atmosphere, and the use and emission of other gases that contribute to the greenhouse effect. Furthermore, we have orchestrated many land-use changes that remove plants, peat bogs, forest and sea grass, which absorb carbon from the atmosphere.

The greenhouse effect

First the positive side of greenhouse gases. They are essential to keeping our planet at a temperature that allows life to thrive; without them heat emitted by the Earth would pass from the Earth's surface into space. This would mean that the Earth would have an average temperature of about $-20°C$.

A greenhouse gas is thus called as it absorbs heat and radiation from the sun. The CO_2 released from the burning of fossil fuels and other activities (the destruction of peat bogs, for example) has accumulated in an insulation blanket that sits around the planet trapping heat in. Anthropogenic sources of CO_2 contribute to enhanced warming – this is warming above and beyond that needed to sustain life. Put simply there aren't the mechanisms or the carbon sinks to deal with the amount of CO_2 we are producing; we are out of balance.

What causes the greenhouse effect? There are number of gases that contribute to the greenhouse effect. The main sources of warming come from the following five gases in order of impact:

- water vapour (H_2O)
- carbon dioxide (CO_2)

- nitrous oxide(N_2O)
- methane (CH_4)
- ozone (O_3)

Each of these gases has a global warming potential (GWP) and has an impact based on the amount of that gas in the atmosphere. For example, although N_2O is 296 times more impactful than CO_2 in terms of GWP, there is significantly more CO_2 in the atmosphere and therefore its impact is greater.

For the majority of the last 800,000 years carbon dioxide concentrations averaged between 200 and 280 ppm. Due to anthropogenic activity this has risen to over 400 ppm.

Based just on the physics of the amount of energy that CO_2 absorbs and emits, a doubling of atmospheric CO_2 concentration relative to pre-industrial levels (up to about 560 ppm) would by itself cause a global average temperature increase of about 1°C.

However, it isn't as simple as this. There are many complex feedback loops and accelerators that we barely understand.

For example, a warmer atmosphere generally contains more water vapour. Water vapour is a really potent greenhouse gas. Therefore, this causes more warming, and therefore water vapour is an amplifier, rather than a driver, of climate change.

Furthermore, as both land and sea ice melts and disappears it exposes darker oceans and land which in turn absorbs more heat from the sun. Interestingly the hole in the ozone layer that emerged due to the use of chlororfluorcarbons

(CFCs) as propellants in aerosols, as degreasers and as refrigerants created a window through which trapped heat could escape. As we have solved this problem now the window will close. This is great news in terms of skin damage and protection from the negative impacts of UV radiation, but it is likely to amplify climate change.

Additionally, warming and increases in water vapour are likely to cause changes in cloud cover which can either amplify or dampen temperature change depending on the properties of the clouds formed. NASA reports that the latest assessment of the science indicates that the overall net global effect of cloud changes is likely to amplify warming.

Then there is the heat dumped into the oceans. NASA estimate that the average ocean temperature has risen by 1°C in the last 100 years with half that rise occurring in the last 30 years.[2]

The oceans have protected us from climate change; they moderate it. They are a significant heat reservoir. Due to the depth of the oceans the heat tends to stay at the top as transfer of warming into deeper oceans is so slow. This transfer rate varies and determines the pace of warming at the surface.

Estimating the rate of global warming is therefore incredibly complex due to the myriad of amplifiers, dampeners, heat stores and complicating factors. Models vary in their projections of how much additional warming to expect but all models are in alignment – they all agree that the overall net effect of the feedback loops is to amplify warming.

2 Biodiversity loss

What is biodiversity? All life on earth.

All life on earth is interconnected in complex and unknown ways. No bees, no plants. No plants, no us. Broken soil (soil is broken – more on that later) equals broken harvests, broken harvests equals no us.

The evidence is stark: without significant changes, 1 million species will be eradicated from the planet. The loss of species and habitats poses as much a danger to life on Earth as climate change does.[3]

According to the above report (see Note 3), biodiversity is collapsing (or declining if you prefer) at a rate that is unprecedented. The IPBES Global Assessment Report on Biodiversity and Ecosystem Services published in 2019 is the most comprehensive ever completed. It is the first intergovernmental report of its kind and its findings are alarming.

The report was compiled by 145 expert authors from 50 countries with inputs from another 310 contributing authors.

It assesses changes over the past five decades, providing a hitherto unknown picture of the relationship between economic development pathways and their impacts on nature.

Furthermore the report attempts to model a number of future scenarios and draws (for the first time ever) upon the knowledge of indigenous populations.

'Biodiversity and nature's contributions to people are our common heritage and humanity's most important life-supporting "safety net". But our safety net is stretched almost to breaking point,' said Professor Sandra Díaz (Argentina), who co-chaired the assessment with Professor Josef Settele

(Germany) and Professor Eduardo S Brondízio (Brazil and the United States). 'The diversity within species, between species and of ecosystems, as well as many fundamental contributions we derive from nature, are declining fast, although we still have the means to ensure a sustainable future for people and the planet.'[4]

WWF have undertaken an analysis of the statistics around biodiversity loss across the planet. The table below summarizes the findings. Each region is analysed and a range of biodiversity loss is estimated. The table shows the median point on that range.

The major reasons for these losses were categorized as:

1 changes in land use, degradation and habitat loss
2 species overexploitation
3 invasive species and disease
4 climate change
5 pollution

TABLE 3.1   Biodiversity loss estimates

Region	Mid-point estimate of loss of biodiversity since 1970
North America	33%
Europe and Central Asia	24%
Latin America and Caribbean	94%
Africa	65%
Asia Pacific	45%

Source: Data taken from WWF Living Planet Report 2020

Here are a couple of 'low-lights' from the report. Three billion animals were displaced or killed in Australia in the 2019 and 2022 bush fires. More than 80 per cent of East and Southeast Asia's wetlands are classified as threatened due to human activity. Illegal hunting and mining have driven down the Grauer's gorilla population in the Congo by 87 per cent (this is particularly important given the value of the DRC rainforest in terms of a carbon sink). In Latin America and the Caribbean in 2019 record-breaking dry seasons and forest fires led to a surge in deforestation, with 30 per cent more than the previous year. In Europe and Central Asia only 23 per cent of species and 16 per cent of its habitats are in good health. In North America 30 per cent of the plant pollination network has disappeared.

Another earlier report found that since 1970 the number of birds, reptiles, mammals and fish on the planet has fallen by 60 per cent.[5] Yep, 60 per cent. Maybe more alarmingly there has been a 75 per cent decline in populations of flying insects (the pollinators) since 1989.[6]

Let's just go back to the premise of this book, that you can't make a profit on a dead planet. With reduced insect populations pollination is harder, maybe impossible. This means that something that was never valued in the equation of product – nature – now has to be turned into a process that costs money (breeding insects specifically to pollinate) and this in turn increases costs and reduces profitability. Absolutely ridiculous. We have rushed to increase yields by using insecticides and pesticides and damaged the very thing that created the yield in the first place. If only someone had warned us about this, eh? Oh that's right, they did. Rachel Carson brought this to the world's attention in her 1962 book *Silent Spring*. But no-one was listening. The warnings went unheeded as they were seen as anti-business. Actually, all this time, the warnings were there to save industry as much as insects. Once again creating a dissonance between ecology and economy damages both and is fundamentally short-sighted and foolish.

Converting biodiversity to profit and removing habitats and developing the land released is the major problem here. However, this will be exacerbated and accelerated by climate change, sea level rises and desertification as each climatic zone flips into the one above. As the old saying goes, 'buy land, they aren't making any more of it'. You can change that to 'buy land, there will be less and less of it'.

3 Ocean health

The oceans cover the majority of the planet, they are not just there for swimming in. They house the ocean currents that redistribute heat around the globe. The Gulf Stream, for example, is the reason that Western Europe is signifi-cantly warmer than it should be due to its latitude. The Gulf Stream originates at the tip of Florida and is a warm ocean current that brings heat swiftly and effectively to Europe. It's a heat conveyor belt. This allows Europe to have the warm (it's all relative) and wet climate that enable its ecosystems and agricultural output. The stability of climate is one of the things that allowed Europe to become established as a population centre due to its ability to feed itself. This in turn led to trade and industry. Without the

Gulf Stream Europe would not have developed in the same way that it did. The oceans have provided climate stability, food, salt and the opportunity to trade. In return we have exploited them, dumped our waste in them and generally abused them. But they've had enough. We currently face a climate emergency, a nature emergency and an ocean emergency. I suspect in that order of importance and urgency. Let's take a look at them briefly now.

If you asked the public what the biggest threat to the oceans is they would have just one answer: plastic. This is of course not the case. While I try not to create league tables of environmental threats, all the reading that I've done on the subject indicates that the greatest threat to the oceans is climate change. Climate change not only raises the temperature of the water and creates migration of species away from the equator; it has a number of other impacts too. Before we look at these it is worth considering the temperature rise first. As mentioned earlier, the average ocean temperature has risen by around 1°C. What does this mean, practically? Here is an anecdotal example. Some 15 years ago I was working for a UK green business support programme called Envirowise (a brilliant initiative that was way ahead of its time). One of the contracts I had was to deliver green business support in Wales. I was asked to go and speak to a fisherman/fish retailer about climate change in Milford Haven. This was at a time when there were still many climate change deniers around and I was worried that I may have to deal with conflict. I approached the client and said: 'Hi there, I'm Mark and I want to talk to you about climate change.'

The client responded with 'Don't talk to me about climate change.' I thought my worst fears were being realized – it was going to be a tricky one. I needn't have worried.

'Climate change is ruining my business,' he continued. 'Its pushing the cod and other stocks further North. I'm having to travel further and be away longer for the same catch. It's pushing prices up and ruining my business. I reckon the sea temperature has risen by two degrees and it's only going to get worse.'

It was a salutary lesson in not pre-judging anyone and another in the business impacts of sustainability collapse. This is the reality: making the same money from the ocean (yep, we can discuss the morality of this later in the book) will be increasingly difficult with migration of (depleting) fish stocks. It was one of the most inspiring conversations I've ever had. Not because it gave scientific hope, but because it gave social hope.

The rising temperatures of the ocean have other impacts. Firstly as the temperature rises the ocean can hold more dissolved carbon dioxide and as there is more carbon dioxide in the atmosphere and more heat this creates a really worrying feedback and amplification loop. Carbon dioxide concentrations in the ocean are higher now than they have been in the last 800,000 years.[7]

But why does acidification matter? The shifting chemical balance and increased acidification is making it hard for shellfish to form their shells and is killing coral reefs (habitats for hundreds of species). This has the potential to destroy the shellfish industry and impact millions of lives and livelihoods. No profit from a dead sea. Ocean acidification has other impacts. Research indicates that as acidity changes many algal species have faster blooms. While this won't damage our health directly it undermines the balance of microscopic life in sea water.

I talked about the Gulf Stream earlier and its importance in stabilizing a friendlier European climate. Well, there are worrying signs that the Gulf Stream itself is being disrupted by climate change. Research from the Potsdam Institute for Climate Impact Research in Germany has identified that the Gulf Stream has two flow states: A fast strong one that has been in place for millennia; and a slow weak one. Data from Potsdam indicates that rising temperatures could make the Gulf Stream oscillate between the two states in as little as 50 years. The implications of this are massive. Niklas Boers of the Institute has identified that global temperature rises have impacted the stability of these currents. The fear is that the Gulf Stream is on the edge of oscillating to the slow-flow state. If this happens there is a significant risk of severe disruption to the rains that billions of people depend on for food in India, South America and West Africa; increasing storms and lowering temperatures in Europe; and pushing up the sea level off eastern North America. There is a fear that it would also further endanger the Amazon rainforest and Antarctic ice sheets. I write this sat in the UK, in a country warmed by the currents of the Gulf Stream, with the thought that with a warming world the climate here could cool significantly (London is further north than Calgary in Canada). Oh the irony, a cooling UK on a warming planet. This is the thing about climate, it is unpredictable and uncertain. The climatic changes we face are lurches, not sequential differences, and this means that planning for them will be incredibly challenging.

Then we have over-fishing and the impact of the fishing industry. The recent film *Seaspiracy* highlighted the negative impact of the fishing industry and overfishing on ocean health. Veteran environmental journalist George Monbiot described it as 'A brilliant expose of the greatest threat to marine life: fishing.' The film is not without its critics, and some of the quotations from the industry and NGOs have been claimed to have been taken out of context. But the main point remains: the fishing industry (over-fishing, by-catch, habitat destruction, discarded fishing equipment) is one of the threats to ocean health and biodiversity. As I say regularly, 'if you really care about the ocean, then stop eating it'. Now clearly there is a question of scale here – hand/line-caught fishing is not the problem. But large-scale commercial fishing, the kind that leaves the seabed bereft of life and results in a high proportion of by-catch (the 'accidental' catching of non-target species) is the problem. It is, literally, the scrubbing of the seabed and this, plus the process by which it is done, is a significant threat to the ocean and its biodiversity.

But let's focus back on plastic. Plastic is an amazing set of materials that has added significantly to food preservation, quality of life and human health and safety. But it's everywhere. It litters the land, sea and even our blood. It's a real and persistent problem. But it isn't the greatest threat to the oceans. That's climate change. Now, the two issues are linked. Not only because plastic is made from oil and oil extraction and processing has a carbon impact (this is true), but because the embedded energy and therefore embedded carbon impact of most of the alternatives to plastic are significantly greater than the carbon impact of plastic. Moving to glass bottles from plastic soft drinks bottles, for example, would increase the carbon impact by up to 500 per cent. While plastic in the environment is a travesty, we may do more harm by switching to what is perceived as a less-damaging material. This area is layered with complexity and emotion. We need to be very clear what problem is the most important to solve. Where should we focus our attention? Now, I agree with the thought bubbling up inside of your head: yes, on both problems; actually all of them. The real issue arises when one solution creates another problem. We will return to this topic later in the book. At this point I just think it is worth saying that there is so much complexity and so much emotion attached to these issues. The interesting thing about the plastic debate is that it is easy to blame someone else rather than examine your own behaviour. The fundamental issue here is the way that we consume, what we consume and how we've allowed convenience to trump common sense.

Other forms of human pollution that are damaging the biodiversity of the oceans include sewage, both human and animal (from animal agriculture); pesticide, herbicide and fertilizer run-off that causes chemical pollution (don't underestimate this, it is considered by many to be one of the most damaging elements of ocean pollution and creates vast dead zones); and air pollution settling on and being absorbed by the oceans.

For centuries we have used the ocean as a dump – in fact we have used nature as a dump. Well, nature has had enough.

4 Ozone depletion

When I graduated in 1992 ozone depletion was the environmental topic everyone knew about. A bit like plastic today. They may not have known what to do about it. A bit like plastic today. They may not have appreciated that the materials in question (CFCs) were nearly perfect. The inventor (Thomas Midgley Jnr) demonstrated their safety by inhaling some then blowing them onto a naked flame, demonstrating their non-toxicity and lack of flammability. He just didn't know about their impact upon the ozone layer. (As an aside Thomas Midgley also invented leaded petrol. He covered up the health impacts of this for years, despite having lead poisoning himself.) People didn't appreciate that their stability in use would create significant problems when they entered the higher levels of the atmosphere. A bit like plastic entering the oceans today.

The impact of CFCs upon the ozone layer was slow, cumulative and lethal. As CFCs rise after use they are broken down by UV radiation (sunlight) and release the chlorine molecules. One chlorine molecule can destroy 100,000 ozone molecules. After 30 years of using CFCs as propellants in aerosols, industrial degreasers and refrigerants enough had been released to have created a hole (well, a very thin patch) in the ozone layer.

The ozone layer protects the planet from harmful UVB radiation that not only causes skin cancers but also damages crops and therefore our ability to feed ourselves.

Through coordinated and collective action starting with the Montreal Protocol in 1987 and the Vienna Convention in 1989, CFCs were removed and alternatives found. Some of those immediate alternatives (HCFCs for example) were more stable but still destroyed the ozone layer over a longer period, so these were then phased out. Replacements for these were wide ranging and generally non-damaging, apart from HFCs (hydrofluorocarbons) which although ozone safe were potent global warmers, so in time these were also phased out.

The point here is that cooperative corporate and political action was harnessed quickly and effectively. We haven't seen the same willingness in terms of climate change and this is for a number of very important reasons:

1 With CFCs there were just a few manufacturers of the gas and hence managing and motivating the supply chain was simpler.

2 The industrial and commercial uses of the gas were far fewer. Literally everything has an embedded, in-use or end-of-life carbon impact. This makes things far harder to regulate.

3 The hard work was done for the consumer/citizen. There was very little, if any, behaviour change required. Drop-in alternative solutions were simply dropped-in. With climate change an entire economic system needs to change; our lifestyles will need to change, and consumption is so closely aligned with our self-worth that we will struggle to shift behaviour.

4 There was no questioning or denying the science of ozone depletion. Climate change denial is a whole industry.

5 Technically, the solutions were (relatively) simple.

6 There were no equity or fairness issues relating to the equalization of global wealth or maintaining a country's resource base.

7 The companies producing the CFCs were going to benefit from inventing and producing alternatives. In the case of climate change there are many vested interests that will be economically hurt by a shift from fossil fuels.

There are, of course, many other environmental challenges but these are the most interesting to me, and the most prescient.

CHAPTER FOUR

Business impacts

The previous chapter looked at the main environmental changes that we are struggling with. Business and the business of consumption drive these. But inside business there can be a focus on the most visible impacts. Indeed, when researching this book I spoke to a business leader who when asked about environmental impact went straight to paper waste rather than climate change. I get it, waste is more tangible. But it is nowhere near the biggest challenge we face. This chapter looks at the things that business would naturally consider as being part of their impact:

- waste
- energy
- resource use

Waste

What is waste?

Waste is a material, substance or by-product eliminated or discarded as no longer useful or required after the completion of a process. Waste is defined by the last user. It isn't waste if it is still useful. In nature there is no waste. Everything breaks down and is absorbed back into nature to be used again. By de-naturing we have created materials that do not break down. I'm not going to bang on about how bad this is, because it isn't. As a species our curiosity has led us to develop amazing materials that have increased our quality of life, saved lives and generally aided social and health progression. But materials in the wrong place, materials surplus to requirement or simply with less economic value than the cost of disposal are written off and defined as waste.

The problem is that non-natural materials accumulate rather than break down. There are two recovery cycles for waste as defined by the Ellen MacArthur Foundation and general circular economy principles; these are the natural cycle and the technical cycle (see Figure 4.1). The natural cycle is the breakdown of materials and re-absorption into nature. The technical cycle is the reprocessing of materials mechanically or chemically for re-use or remanufacture. Let's dig into these a little.

Biological cycle

The biological cycle sees the return of bio-based materials back into nature or back into the manufacturing process.

FIGURE 4.1   The two cycles of the circular economy

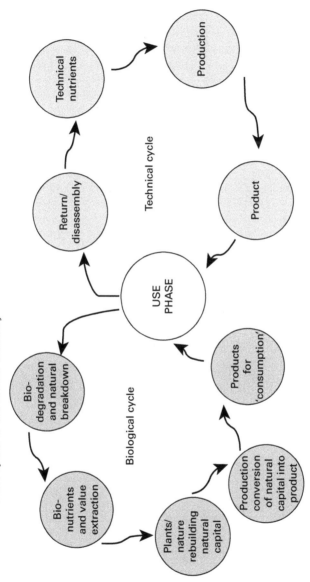

Additionally, the breakdown of bio materials can give rise to methane and other gases. These are then used to generate energy. The main tenet of circularity is that the materials used are really only being borrowed from nature and will make their way back into nature. The chemicals that make up the materials are returned back into natural cycles such as the carbon cycle, the phosphorous cycle and the nitrogen cycle.

It is important to acknowledge that these natural cycles are very long. They take years to complete and hence removing and using materials faster than they can regenerate is not circular. Our extraction of fossil fuels and conversion into power and carbon dioxide faster than the planet can recycle that carbon dioxide into plants and soils is a case in point. We've actually exacerbated the problems in this cycle by destroying soil structure and depending upon agricultural methods that diminish soil carbon. More on this later.

Most of the natural cycles are not functioning effectively at the moment due to the way that we have extracted materials and then disposed of them. We will look at this when we consider regenerative agriculture.

It is also worth noting that many materials developed to slip into the natural cycle (and in particular compostable plastics) do not perform well in terms of biodegradation unless they are put into industrial, in-vessel composting systems. Furthermore, if these materials are confused with traditional plastics and enter the technical cycle they create havoc within the plastic recycling stream as they melt at lower temperatures and mess up the intrusion or extrusion process. They are incredibly hard to differentiate from 'normal' plastics and we have poor reprocessing processes in place worldwide.

Technological cycle

The technological cycle is, as described, the technological recovery of materials back into secondary materials that can be used again. It is important to pause here and say that recycling and chemical recycling are really last resorts.

FIGURE 4.2   Circular economy design models, as conceived by The Great Recovery

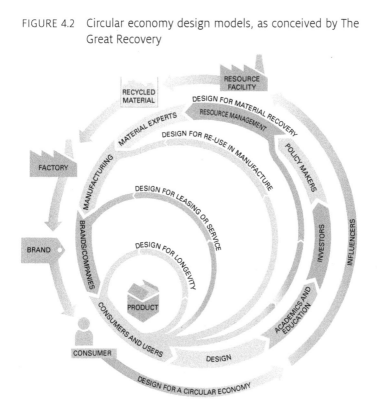

Re-use, refurbishment and parts donation should all come first. Only when the product has no viable practical re-use option should it go for technical recycling.

One of the pieces of work that I am most proud to have been involved with is a circular economy project run by The Royal Society for the Encouragement of Arts, Manufactures and Commerce, also known as the Royal Society of Arts or more commonly by its acronym RSA. The project was called The Great Recovery and was led by Sophie Thomas. I built and delivered the workshop activity for the project. The communications were beautiful and clearly demonstrated the refurbishment and re-use option ahead of technical recycling. These are shown in Figure 4.2.

As previously stated my favourite circular economy strategy is longevity. Keeping a product going for as long as possible is usually the best environmental option due to embedded impact in the materials. However, this isn't the case for energy-using products.

Making these measures mean something

Calculating the environmental impact per use/per wear is a great way of understanding whole life environmental (and financial) costs. A good example here is artisan denim. Let me explain. There are many artisan denim companies around the globe. My favourites are Black Horse Lane, Dawson and Hiut. All three offer free repairs for life. This makes their jeans the cheapest jeans you can buy over their (and your) lifetime. The purchase price is high ($150–200 a pair) but over the lifetime of the jeans (let's estimate 15 years and $180 a pair) this is around $12 a year. Compare that to a pair of standard (and perfectly good) pair of Levis 501s. These are around $80 a pair on the web. But if you've not got $80 you would need to buy them from a catalogue where they are $120 for the same jeans, and you would tick the box that says 'pay weekly'. This is at an APR of 39.9 per cent. Therefore, over a year you will pay $180 for the same jeans that most people pay $80 for. But how long will these last? The average lifespan for a pair of jeans, according to the International Fabric Institute Fair Claims Guide, is two to three years. Let's assume three years. That gives a price per year of $60, versus $12 a year for the 'repaired free for life' jeans.

This highlights that the challenge with well-made and long-lasting products is one of fairness, equity and business models. The wealthy get better value. Furthermore, as one of the main challenges we face is how we make more or the same profit from selling fewer things, longevity and higher quality products allow this to happen but disenfranchise the less wealthy. One of the main barriers to the development of circular economy products and services is the need for better business models.

An extension of this thinking brings us to products that have been designed for leasing or service. In order to be leased over a long period the items need to be designed for longevity. But they also need to be designed for speed and ease of repair; this often means that they will be designed in a modular way to enable parts/components to be swapped out quickly and cheaply. Xerox pioneered this thinking back in the late 1980s with their pay-to-print model where copy and print machines were leased and the customer paid per sheet printed. Xerox then owned the units and refurbished and serviced them regularly. For a different market (the consumer market) Dyson have simplified and modularized the design of their vacuum cleaners so that hoses and brushes can be unclipped and clipped back in easily and motors can be switched out quickly. This elongates the length of life and reduces the environmental impact per year of ownership and cost of ownership.

Designing for re-use in manufacture develops products or their components that can be taken back by business to be re-used or re-built for re-sale. This system sees the product go back to the manufacturer for refurbishment/remanufacture rather than staying with the consumer.

Then and only then does the product enter the technical recovery cycle.

Consumer waste or business waste?

Waste arises for many reasons and we tend to judge the amount of waste we produce at the consumer level, whereas waste has been produced all along the supply chain. This is inefficient in a number of ways. Let's look at the food production, distribution and retail supply chain for greater detail.

In the UK, food waste totals 9.5 million tonnes with 70 per cent of this occurring in citizens' homes.[1] However, as someone who has worked in food retail (I was the Environmental Manager at the supermarket Asda in 2000–01) I am particularly aware of food that is wasted before it hits the retailer shelves, and the figure above excludes that waste. WWF found a whopping 3.3 million tonnes of food is wasted on UK farms each year. This is due to a number of reasons. A key one is food being 'out of specification' for the retailer. This includes fresh produce being too large or too small (supermarkets specify the perfect apple diameter for example and anything outside of this approved range is scrapped – crazy, eh?), animals being too large or too small, eggs being the wrong size/weight or having visual imperfections on the shell. There are many more examples; this isn't just about wonky vegetables. At a time of food shortages, a cost-of-living crisis, malnutrition twinned with obesity (our food is calorie rich but nutrient deficient) it seems unbelievable that our retail systems are the cause of such high levels of waste. At 3.3 million tonnes of food waste per year this means that pre-retailer waste is 25 per cent of all food waste.

Frankly I suspect that this is an underestimate. I have seen previous valuations that a third of the food we produce is lost pre-retailer (this is from a now unavailable 2013 report by the UK Institute of Mechanical Engineers and was reported in the *Guardian* newspaper.[2]

But let's be cautious here and say that 25 per cent of all food waste is on-farm. The sources of the other 75 per cent are complex and range from our desire to have all produce available to buy all the time (this places the retailer in the difficult position of having to have enough food in stock but not too much), inflexible supplier contracts and specifications, promotions and encouragement to buy more (this is not all bad news, however; promotions and buy-one-get-one-frees are a great ways of dealing with seasonal gluts and bumper harvests, although they do encourage over-purchasing), the consumer's over-purchasing, poor meal planning and poor left-over utilization. There are a number of skills and systems that need to be improved here and these are not just with the consumer.

Food waste is particularly important as it has a high global warming potential (GWP). GWP figures convert the carbon and methane (and other gases) emissions from a product (all the way from cradle to grave) producing a figure for its climate impact. It is easy to see this as just the methane generated as the produce breaks down. This is indeed significant as methane is a potent global warming gas (methane has 80 times the GWP of CO_2 over 20 years). But the GWP also includes the whole production process from planting, chemical fertilizer use and harvesting, to processing, packaging and distribution. This mounts up and demonstrates the need to use food wisely. This is particularly true of any product that has animal produce in it, whether that be meat or dairy. On a trip to the United States once I was awarded 'guest of the week' by the hotel (I genuinely have no idea what I did to deserve this). The reward was a bottle of local beer and a Danish pastry. I snapped a photograph and put it on Instagram (like you do). The pastry was covered over with some cling film to stop it going off. I received one comment from someone who professes to be an environmental expert criticizing the hotel for use of plastic wrap. Clearly I understand the need to use less plastic and to treat it correctly post-use, but the point here is that the impact of a small piece of cling film (weighing less than 1 g in this case) has a carbon impact of 2 g carbon dioxide equivalent (CO_2e). Whereas the carbon impact of a pastry is circa 300 g carbon. This demonstrates the point that embedded carbon is often invisible while we focus on the totems of 'being good'. There should be no confusion here: the biggest threats to humankind are climate change and biodiversity loss. In nearly all situations (apart from regenerative agriculture which we will discuss later) current animal agriculture exacerbates both. Therefore preserving the pastry beats wasting the 1 g of cling film, massively.

Sometimes in our rush to improve the situation we cling to totems rather than science. This is not helpful. Science should lead, always.

All of this highlights the importance of understanding the true impact of the products we make and therefore the impact of the waste we produce. Waste is only waste if we decide it is so. Keeping things going longer is the key to reducing waste. This doesn't always fit with our model of capitalism – we will return to this theme later.

It's also about the downstream

Waste isn't just a waste of resources, it also creates many other downstream impacts.

Traditionally waste has been dumped in a hole in the ground or burned. Both have knock-on environmental consequences. We throw things away, but 'away' has gone away. Holes in the ground used to be cheap and plentiful: they aren't cheap anymore. This is partially down to the environmental regulations that they have to meet and partially down to landfill tax that is applied to most wastes. This tax has been applied in order to incentivize options other than landfill. This is in line with the waste hierarchy which prioritizes waste avoidance (reduction), re-use, recycling then disposal (see Figure 4.3). On environmental

FIGURE 4.3   The waste hierarchy

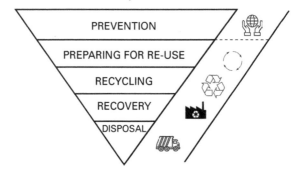

grounds incineration with energy recovery is preferred to landfill as there is a degree of value extraction.

What are the impacts of landfilling waste?

Out of sight, out of mind is how we've thought about waste for decades. However, it's not the last we see of it. Waste has a significant half-life. If it is able to break down in landfill it will release CO_2, methane and other gases that have deleterious effects. A report from the International Solid Waste Association[3] estimates that landfill sites could be responsible for 10 per cent of all greenhouse gas emissions by 2050. If landfilled waste has damaging chemicals in it these can leach out and into water sources and contaminate land. Of particular concern is mercury from lighting products and lead stripped off electrical products by acidic rain. Additionally there are risks of leachate (the liquid soup released from things as they break down) escaping into water courses and into the water table. Modern landfills are exceptionally well designed and need to meet very stringent design criteria in terms of leachate collection and treatment, apart from leachate from sites that take 'inert' waste; this doesn't need to be collected or treated. All other landfills require lining, drainage, pumping and treatment in the UK and EU. They also require landfill gas extraction and management as a part of their permission to operate. Older landfills, however, are still off-gassing and still leaking. The shifting of taxation onto landfill in most industrialized countries has ensured that the focus has moved from landfill to alternative methods of treatment. There is a dark side to this shift, however. Much plastic waste in particular is exported to emerging economies such as Turkey where it is intended for recycling facilities. However, there is significant and growing evidence that exported plastic waste is not recycled but is either dumped or burnt resulting in significant environmental damage.[4]

The problem with exporting waste to countries that may not treat it in line with best practice is that this waste ends up in places that it shouldn't. Let's take plastic as an example. Despite being a great packaging material for some products it is the 'enfant terrible' of the materials world as it is incredibly persistent and it floats. Recent research has highlighted that 10 river systems are responsible for between 85 and 99 per cent of all land-based plastic that enters the oceans from rivers. The problem isn't the material, it is the lack of appropriate systems to deal with it.

Ostensibly, we are trying to solve the problem by sending materials for recycling, and sending them for recycling in the parts of the world where the polymer is likely to be used again (Asia). This makes sense logistically, but by so doing we can end up making things worse. It is important to remember that there is no such thing as bad materials, there are just bad systems.

One such poorly designed system is the incineration (with energy recovery) system. In Europe these are, generally, built as a public–private sector partnership. This means they are built and financed by the private sector for the benefit of the public sector who pay a fee to use them. It shifts the financing from capital cost into revenue cost. The problem here is that they are usually built against the backdrop of a contract that specifies a certain amount of material going through them each year. As we have increased the amount of material going to recycling this has left less waste going to incineration. But the local authority will have a contract to send a certain weight of material to incineration (with energy recovery). If these contractual obligations are not met there is a resulting financial penalty. Consequently, there is a need to 'feed' these waste to energy facilities and a growing risk that, to avoid financial penalties, materials will be pulled from the circular economy, from recycling, into incineration.

What are the impacts of incineration?

Let's stay with incineration (with energy recovery) for a short while.

Waste incineration is the burning of residual waste (waste that is not recycled or composted) to make electricity (energy from waste), and has been championed by some as one of the keys to reducing carbon emissions from waste treatment (and also electricity production). However, recent research by Eunomia (commissioned by ClientEarth) has indicated that incineration with energy recovery cannot be considered a low-carbon energy over a 15-year period and in terms of disposal will become more carbon intensive than landfilling by 2035.

Furthermore, there are concerns regarding the gases that are emitted from the process. The main gases emitted from these facilities are volatile organic compounds (VOCs), PM2.5 (these are very small particles that are able to pass into the lungs), sulphur dioxide (SOx) and nitrogen dioxide (NOx).

I will look at each in turn.

VOCs are a group of chemicals found in many products. These compounds easily become vapours when burnt. They have health implications on their own but when combined with Nitrogen Oxides can form ozone. Ozone is comprised of three oxygen molecules and causes breathing and respiratory health problems for the young, the old and anyone with an existing lung condition. Exposure to VOCs has been shown to cause a variety of health concerns including: eye, nose, and throat irritation; headache, loss of coordination, nausea; and damage to the liver, kidneys or central nervous system. Scary huh? Additionally some VOCs are suspected or proven carcinogens.

PM2.5. The air that we breathe isn't just gas. It contains tiny fragments of solids too. These include carbon, dust, chemicals, smoke, plastic, soot, brake-linings and tyre dust. Anything that is below two and a half microns in size. These particles are not only invisible to the eye but are small enough to pass into the lungs, and through the lungs into your blood and organs. There is also an increasing body of evidence linking PM2.5s with dementia[5] and Parkinson's disease.[6]

Our exposure to PM2.5s is high but falling. Most governments set targets of 20 µg/m3 but the World Health Organization target is 5 µg/m3. While exposure levels are falling they aren't falling fast enough with 6 per cent of UK adult deaths linked to PM2.5s each year, down from 7 per cent in 2018 (the pandemic shutdown saw a significant drop in these emissions). More detail can be found on the Public Health England site.[7]

SOx has an impact upon human health through inhalation. It can have the following effects: wheezing, shortness of breath and chest tightness, especially during exercise. Continued exposure at high levels increases respiratory symptoms and reduces the ability of the lungs to function. Short exposures can make it difficult for people with asthma to breathe when they are active outdoors. SOx can reach the lower respiratory tract through rapid or deep breathing. Exposure brings with it the increased risk of hospital admissions, especially among the vulnerable.

NOx is a gaseous air pollutant composed of nitrogen and oxygen. It forms when fossil fuels or waste is burned at high temperatures. Nitrogen oxides in the outdoor air contribute to particle pollution and to the chemical reactions that make ozone. Exposure brings a greater risk of asthma, respiratory problems, wheezing and decreased lung function.

So, all in all, not nice.

Environmental impacts of incinerators

The social impacts are pretty grim, but at least we are getting rid of stuff and generating electricity at the same time, right? Well, hold your horses. It's not as simple as that. While we might think that any kind of value recovery beats no value recovery, it all depends on the other side of the equation. Yes value recovery is to be welcomed but not if the process does harm.

Firstly, the gaseous emissions discussed above have environmental impacts too. SOx and rain water can create weak sulphuric acid which has negative impacts on water courses, soil, vegetation and the (already acidifying) oceans. This has knock-on impacts on flora and fauna. Furthermore, at high concentrations SOx has negative impacts upon vegetation growth and plant health. NOx too reduces crop growth and yields.

In terms of particulate matter (the PM2.5s), the negative environmental impacts are significant. They have been shown to adversely affect climate and ecosystems, and also materials used to build cities, infrastructure and the products we use. In terms of climate change some elements (black carbon) enhance climate warming while others (nitrate and sulphate) have a cooling impact. Additionally, they negatively impact plant growth (and therefore harvest and yields) and water quality.

VOCs are not great either. They have harmful effects on the environment through toxicity, damage to materials, tropospheric photochemical oxidant formation, stratospheric ozone depletion and global climate change. The latter is worth dwelling upon.

By absorbing infrared radiation from the earth's surface, almost all VOCs contribute to global heating. The more complex a VOC, the greater its propensity to absorb infrared radiation. However, most VOCs have a short atmospheric lifetime and are dissolved, which reduces their impact (the exceptions to this rule are saturated light hydrocarbons and halogenated compounds). Additionally, VOCs alter ozone concentrations, a potent greenhouse gas which causes indirect global warming.

Yes, incineration with energy recovery does indeed generate energy, but the carbon benefits of this are increasingly being questioned when compared to recycling.

Incineration rates have risen steadily over the last 20 years and that, in turn, has negative implications. Rates have risen from under 10 per cent of waste collected in the UK in 2001 to almost 50 per cent of municipal waste collected in 2020/21.[8]

Interestingly in those areas with high incineration rates the recycling rates are lower. Removing value in one way (calorific) means that the real value, the atoms, no longer has the potential to be used again and again. This is demonstrated from the same dataset from the UK and demonstrates the point made above regarding the need to feed these beasts once they are built. These contracts can be 30 years plus in length.

As I've said before, 'away' has gone away. 'Away' was only cheap because the true external costs of social and environmental impact were never accounted for. That is changing, and while we can chase cheaper labour and lower environmental regulations around the globe, in the end we will need to pay more for better. This challenges the current version of capitalism and asks the question how do we redesign it to place people and planet on a par with profit.

Energy

We take energy for granted, at least in the Global North and West. We simply flick a switch or turn a dial and the product we are using springs into life. It was the harnessing of energy creation that heralded the industrial revolution. Initially all energy was renewably generated by water power. The conversion of movement to power was a mechanical process. With no electrical power and no electrical light people worked when the sun was up or under candle light. Water was warmed by fire. Business used the same methods to create light and heat, but this didn't effectively scale. It was the discovery of electricity that really saw things start to heat up (pun intended). This was intertwined with the industrial revolution. One stimulated the other. The conversion of coal to steam and steam to manufacturing power was the key. The inventor James Watt built (with others) the first coal-powered steam engine that converted coal to power more quickly and with greater power output than using previous fuels (such as wood and peat). Traditional biomass (the burning of solid fuels like wood, crop waste or charcoal) was the world's main source of energy up until the middle of the 19th century. The astounding rise of coal fuelled the industrial revolution. This saw the acceleration of fossil fuels as the source of manufacturing power. Table 4.1 shows the way that primary power sources have changed over time.

As with all environmental impacts the type of pollution is only one factor; the compounding factor is really the scale at which it is used/emitted. This is down to the

TABLE 4.1   Global energy consumption by energy source TWh

Source	1800	1850	1900	1950	2021
Traditional biomass	5,556	7,222	6,111	7,500	11,111
Coal	97	569	5,728	12,603	41,964
Oil	0	0	181	5,444	51,170
Natural gas	0	0	64	2,092	40,375
Nuclear	0	0	0	0	7,031
Hydropower	0	0	47	925	11,183
Wind	0	0	0	0	4,872
Solar	0	0	0	0	2,702
Modern biofuels	0	0	0	0	1,140
Other renewables	0	0	0	0	2,373

Source: UKWIN (2023) Facts and figures, https://ukwin.org.uk/facts

explosion of population and the advent of mass production and consumption that resulted in a booming use of energy.

The range of power sources expanded during the 20th century. First oil, gas, then hydropower. In the 1960s nuclear energy was added to the mix. The sources that are likely to power the future, renewables – solar, wind and tidal – were only added much later, in the 1980s.

TABLE 4.2   Electricity production by source 1980–2021 TWh

Source	1980	1990	2000	2010	2021
Coal	3,748	4,460	5,719	8,364	10,086
Oil	1,109	1,365	1,173	953	764
Natural gas	1,426	1,790	2,718	4,753	6,338
Nuclear	1,489	2,000	2,507	2,686	2,739
Hydropower	1,980	2,159	2,621	3,412	4,234
Wind	0	4	31	346	1,848
Solar	0	0	1	31	1,041
Modern biofuels	0	0	148	324	666
Other renewables	0	0	52	69	96
Total	9,752	11,778	14,970	20,938	27,812

This expansion of sources can be seen in Table 4.2. This data comes from the brilliant ourworldindata.org which really is an amazing set of resources.

The things to note here are the decline of coal and its replacement with natural gas. This was thought of as a transition fuel but in reality its use slowed down the development of renewables.

That's all fine and dandy but it is the past. I have a saying 'data is great but it is already history. We need to know what will happen tomorrow. Don't play soccer where the ball is, play where the ball is going to be.' So where are we headed?

The first element to consider here is the existing global energy reserves. Then we will look at projected demand.

Global energy reserves

Using ourworldindata.org as a source the remaining known reserves (at 2020 consumption rates) are:

- coal: 139 years
- oil: 54 years
- gas: 49 years

The problem is that if we are to have any chance of keeping global warming to below 2°C we need to leave the remaining fossil fuels in the ground. Those governments that have signed up to the Paris Agreement (the Paris Agreement is a legally binding international treaty on climate change adopted by 196 parties at COP21 in Paris, on 12 December 2015; it aims to limit global warming to well below 2°C, ideally to 1.5°C, relative to pre-industrial levels. In order to meet this, countries need to reach a global peak of greenhouse gas emissions as soon as possible to achieve a climate neutral world by mid-century) have not established target dates to stop burning fossil fuels, indeed many countries (the UK included) are still granting planning permission for new coal mines. The urgency is the output of burning fossil fuels rather than the availability, although the end of that is also in sight.

Of course, there is no shortage of solar, wind or tidal. However, there are concerns relating to material availability for renewable energy systems. Of particular concern is lithium and cobalt for batteries and neodymium for the magnets in turbines. There is less concern regarding the amount that is available in the world and more concern about the geopolitics (who owns it and will they let it be traded), the labour conditions associated with mining and processing the materials, and the economic value given high and expanding demand.

Energy demand projections

Projecting demand for energy has always been challenging. SP Global, a commodity insights specialist, predict that global energy demand will grow by 47 per cent by 2050, with oil being the largest source of energy. This is terrifying. However, the good news is that the faster growing element of the energy mix is renewables with a project growth rate of 165 per cent compared to a growth rate in liquid fuels (oil) of 36 per cent. Energy-related carbon emissions are set to continue to rise at a time when we need them to reduce. The data is unpredictable on carbon emissions and much depends on the energy mix as discussed above. With business as usual, the OECD predict that energy-related CO_2 emissions will rise by 70 per cent.[9]

This would see atmospheric CO_2 concentrations hit 686 ppm and global average temperatures hit between 3 and 6°C. If we take action, and particularly if we de-carbonize energy, then we can restrict temperature rises to around 2°C.

Resource use

If you don't own stuff, you can't make things. I talked about the equation of production earlier and how resource availability is crucial to capitalism, to consumerism, to enhancing quality of life, but the preserving of resources is essential in terms of intergenerational equity.

There is an important discussion about fairness here. This debate gave rise to the concept of Earth Overshoot Day. We currently use the equivalent of 1.7 Earths, this means that we are using resources up 1.7 times faster than the planet can regenerate them. Some countries are using them way faster than that. The United States, for example, uses resources five times faster than they regenerate. The reason this is currently achievable is that we borrow from the future and the use of resources is not fairly distributed geographically.

The website overshootday.org goes into greater detail. It takes the global resource-use data and identifies a day each year when we have used our notional fair share of resources. It does so for the world as a whole and for each country. The assumptions and the science that sits behind this are detailed but the thing that interests me is the change over time. We are hitting our overshoot day earlier each year. Between 1971 and 2022 the offshoot day has moved from late December to late July.

The thing that interests me is the trend. It's a galloping trend. The amount of resources we use each year is increasing and the proportion of the world that is considered 'developed' is also increasing. These two trends are likely to be compounded by a third trend, that of increasing population numbers. However, the global population is set to begin reducing from the end of this century.

Projections from the UN indicate that despite current growth the global population will level out around 2086, and some sources predict the start of a decline before then. The main reason for this is a drop in global total fertility rate. It has dropped from 5.3 in 1963 to 2.4 in 2019. There are a number of commentators expressing concern that this rate of depopulation will become a significant challenge. There is a now famous conversation between Elon Musk and Jack Ma about this subject. Links don't work well in books but please do search it out on the web.

When it comes to resource availability the human race is ingenious and is able to innovate away from scarce materials and develop products that use a more flexible and broader range of materials. But scarcity is, as we have already seen, not just down to absolute availability. Perhaps the main challenge in terms of resource scarcity is who owns the resources and who controls access to them. We've covered the geopolitics of this earlier but I can't emphasize enough how important this is. Having control over access to resources and labour allows businesses or economies to control the market. We saw this in 2022 when the supply of semiconductor chips and car parts as a result of the pandemic was constrained. Availability of parts, components and ultimately the final product shifted the value of used vehicles up by 9.2 per cent in one quarter alone. As soon as materials stop flowing into an economy it sparks a panic and demand spikes, thereby exacerbating the situation. It isn't just global pandemics that bring on resource shortages; there are significant concerns of market manipulation through price dropping. This fear is focused on China as their investment in resource-rich but cash-poor economies is famous (and smart). So-called rare earth elements (REEs) and rare earth oxides (REOs) are not actually that rare but they are very difficult and expensive to extract. REOs make up only around 0.01 per cent of the total tonnage of non-fuel minerals produced, but even though the global REE market is small, their significance for a wide range of strategic technologies cannot be overstated. The 17 elements that make up the REE group are really quite widespread, although challenging to extract due to their characteristic low concentration in many ores and quick oxidation. In a wide range of high-tech end-use applications, REE are essential. These include typical household gadgets like digital cameras, PCs and mobile phones with built-in cameras. Renewable energy production and defence are particularly impacted by REE sensitivity. If you own access to resources then you own the future.

There's a great paper by The Baker Institute at Rice University in the United States that demonstrates the current state of play in terms of rare earth ownership and processing.[10] The demand for rare earths is increasing rapidly and much of this is driven by environmental technologies such as battery energy storage and sintered magnets for electric vehicles, turbines and other electronics.

The interesting observation that can be extracted here is that the big increases in demand are in catalysts and magnets (the latter mainly for turbines, electric motors and other elements of renewable power generation). For example, demand for magnets is predicted to double by 2025 compared to 2019 figures.

According to estimates published by Statista, China's reserves of REE amounted to an estimated **44 million** metric tonnes. The same paper estimates that there are **120 million** metric tonnes of REE in existence. The location of these materials can be seen in Table 4.3.

In terms of the mining of these materials, Table 4.4 shows the dominance of China's REE extraction industry.

TABLE 4.3   Rare earth production and reserves

Country	Mine production 2020	Reserves	% of total reserves
China	140,000	44,000,000	38.0%
Vietnam	1,000	22,000,000	19.0%
Brazil	1,000	21,000,000	18.1%
Russia	2,700	12,000,000	10.4%
India	3,000	6,900,000	6.0%
Australia	17,000	4,100,000	3.5%
United States	38,000	1,500,000	1.3%
Greenland	–	1,500,000	1.3%
Tanzania	–	890,000	0.8%
Canada	–	830,000	0.7%
South Africa	–	790,000	0.7%
Other Countries	100	310,000	0.3%

(continued)

TABLE 4.3   (Continued)

Country	Mine production 2020	Reserves	% of total reserves
Burma	30,000	N/A	N/A
Madagascar	8,000	N/A	N/A
Thailand	2,000	N/A	N/A
Burundi	500	N/A	N/A

TABLE 4.4   Share of Global REE extraction by country

Country	Percentage share
China	60.63
United States	15.52
Myanmar	9.38
Australia	7.94
Thailand	2.89
Madagascar	1.15
India	1.05
Russia	0.97
Brazil	0.18
Vietnam	0.14
Burundi	0.04

What does all this mean? Well, the means of production are disproportionately important to the economic prosperity and the stability of nations. When the world's supply chains are controlled by one or two major economies this creates strategic economic threats. During periods of relative calm, China would be reluctant to impose restrictions on the supply of rare earths for solely political reasons. They are restricted in their ability to decrease exports while preserving local output by a 2014 World Trade Organization (WTO) judgement. In addition, supply interruptions would make them less dominant as the West creates substitutes and further develops sources within their or allies' control. However, China may be tempted to restrict rare earth exports given their ultimate applications in defence technologies, power production and other key items in the event of a military confrontation between the US and China – something which is becoming increasingly possible given hotspots like Taiwan. Chinese officials are now better able to implement and enforce production and export limitations, manipulating pricing in a way that benefits them, thanks to the recently unified rare earth business and the sovereign-owned China Rare Earth Group.

But what about the sustainability implications? The extraction and processing of any material has negative environmental implications. But as previously noted the extraction of rare earths is complicated not by their scarcity but by the difficulty of extraction. They tend to exist in low concentrations and this means that they are costly and inefficient to mine as it is necessary to remove and process a lot of material per kg of rare earth. Furthermore, we are seeing increasing interest is chemical extraction. According to a paper in the journal *Scientific Reports*,[11] mining is the most significant activity destroying the ecological environment and causing pollution and environmental disasters. Extraction damages water bodies, the atmosphere, soil, fauna and flora. Furthermore, mining effluent can result in the acidification of soil and groundwater and other mining wastes can cause heavy metal and radioactive contamination.

Due to the rush to achieve net-zero goals we have created an increased demand for REE and this has led to a bottleneck of elements such as cobalt, copper and lithium. These are essential to producing renewable energy technology, from electric vehicle batteries to wind turbine blades.

Let's look at just one of these, cobalt. The world's greatest cobalt reserves, estimated to be 4 million metric tonnes as of 2022, are in the Democratic Republic of the Congo (DRC). The cobalt reserves in the DRC make up about half of the world's total reserves, which total 8.3 million metric tonnes. The next largest reserves are held by Australia, with 1.5 million metric tonnes. We aren't able to fully understand or estimate the scale of the reserves of REEs in Africa. Cobalt is extracted as a by-product from mining copper and nickel. Only 2 per cent is mined on its own. This makes calculating an environmental impact exceptionally difficult as the same process is producing two products. However, the Cobalt Institute estimate that the impact per kg of metal is 28.2 kg CO_2e. This is high. However, the benefit of using the metal over its lifetime will dramatically outweigh the impact of extraction and manufacture but it does underline the need to be lean and to capture waste cobalt and cobalt from waste products.

This example demonstrates the challenges we face in making the best environmental decisions. Extraction and use will have a significant benefit environmentally, one that outweighs its environmental impact.

Additionally, we have built materials recycling targets based upon weight. This is important, an important error as it incentivizes the recovery of the main mass of an electrical product which is likely to be a less precious material (plastic, maybe steel) rather than the lighter materials in smaller quantities that have greater environmental (and financial) value. We need to recover value not mass. Weight-based targets point us in the wrong direction.

We have the periodic table in our hand when we hold waste products; we are letting it slip through our fingers.

CHAPTER FIVE

Is there any good news?

Against a backdrop of environmental concern it is no surprise that people feel overwhelmed. The terms 'climate anxiety' and 'eco anxiety' have entered common parlance. This is a symptom of the language used to communicate the urgent position we find ourselves in. Correction – it is a symptom of the urgent position we find ourselves in. After 40 years of trying to increase awareness, of trying to wake up the population and business, the environmental sector has resorted to alarm. This is entirely understandable. When no-one listens the tendency is to shout louder. Then that shout, that cry of alarm, gets picked up by the media (it is important to remember that good news rarely, if at all, sells newspapers or clicks) and we get a spiralling of alarm. This gives rise to two reactions.

The first is climate scepticism. It seems hard to believe but market researchers IPSOS have identified an increase in those being sceptical about climate claims of 6 per cent (rising from 31 to 37 per cent) in the three years up to 2022.[1]

The second is a rise in climate anxiety. A 2020 survey of psychiatrists in England found that 57 per cent are seeing children and young people distressed about the climate and environment.[2] And this is not just a UK or EU phenomena. The largest and widest geographic research into young people's anxiety around climate change found that climate anxiety is profoundly affecting young people around the globe, but that respondents from the Global South (maybe more likely to have witnessed change) were most concerned.[3] The most striking finding from this work is that this research is the first to identify feelings of abandonment and betrayal by governments and the adult world generally. The mental health implications from living in fear, to abandonment, conflict avoidance and resignation are significant barriers to collective action and may hinder our ability to respond, and the speed of response. The existential nature and time delay of the climate change threat also gets in the way of action. There is an urgent need for governments to develop and stick to a coordinated strategy, to assist business in redefining the way it makes money and a shift in the tax and subsidy mechanisms that, frankly, are exacerbating the continued extraction and burning of fossil fuels.

But there is some good news. There are people and organizations making progress, developing approaches that are improving things and in so doing creating the conditions for sustainable profits. We're going to look at some of these now. It's not an exhaustive list; there are great people and good businesses everywhere. Look for the light rather than the dark.

What are the things that give me hope, that are beginning to change the way we make profit?

1 The energy revolution

I say energy. I mean electricity. Gas and oil can only be burnt to give rise to heat. Electricity can be generated in many ways and those electrons generated can be used in many, many ways. For example, we have seen a boom in solar production due to improved technology, the tumbling price of solar panels and some government subsidies.

In 2010 the world produced 32.2 TWh of solar electricity. By 2021 we were producing 1,003 TWh. That's roughly a 3,000 per cent growth in 11 years. Pretty good, eh? Yes, but if we are to hit net zero impact of energy production the world will need to produce 7,500 TWh per year by 2030. That's soon. It requires a 25 per cent annualized growth in capacity. The good news here is that is indeed the rate at which solar production has grown over the last five years. We can do this, with solar alone (back to this in a moment). While large-scale solar production is essential (it makes up around half of the solar power we currently produce) there is a need to accelerate distributed production. Small-scale and house-scale production make up the other half. This is where continued incentives are important to entice businesses to place solar on their rooftops. Clearly to do this the business needs to own the building and hence there will always be a need for offset-based solar production, as not all businesses can produce it themselves. But those businesses that can invest in direct solar production, indeed in renewables generally, will see their energy costs tumble. But fear not, if you have no rooftop you can still cash in on this opportunity. Recent research by Bloomberg has shown that the return on investment in renewable power stocks produced a 426 per cent return since 2010.[4] This is triple the return achieved on investment in fossil fuel companies. Why then do we persist in subsidizing the fossil fuel industry? In 2021 the International Energy Authority estimated that governmental subsidies for the fossil fuel industry reached $1 trillion.[5] That is double the 2020 figure. In the same year the level of governmental support for renewable energy was $480 billion.[6] Let's just re-cap: renewables deliver greater profit and return on investment; renewables are close to net zero (there is an embedded impact in panel production and energy transfer); renewables need very little maintenance and operational budget. Yet governments persist in throwing twice as much money at a dying, inefficient, polluting and planet-ending industry as it does at renewables. Makes no sense, right? My message is pick a side, back yourself and the sectors that do more good than bad, and change the economic model that supports energy. Yes, there will be job losses. I don't say that blithely. This is scary and its one of the sticks that the fossil fuel industry hit governments with over the last 10 years. But there are now more jobs associated with renewables than with fossil fuels[7] and there is an estimated need to create another 14 million by 2030 and move another 16 million to clean energy roles. There are 65 million jobs in the energy sector and between 2019 and 2021 virtually all the new jobs created have been in renewables. We need to stop talking about transition fuels, stop fixating on tapering-off fossil fuels, take our foot off the brake and properly support the renewables sector. Michael Liebreich of Bloomberg recently outlined the scale of the opportunity.[8] Just focusing on heat he predicts it will become the next half trillion dollar market. This is just for heat. We have the potential to do this using clean electrons (generated from renewable sources) or dirty electrons (generated from fossil fuels).

Of course, solar is just one way of generating green electrons. Wind power has seen unprecedented growth over the last 10 years. In 2021 alone it increased by 17 per cent and generated 1870 TWh that year. This is great but growth needs to continue at a rate of 18 per cent between 2022 and 2030 in order to hit net zero targets. China leads the way here being responsible for 70 per cent of wind generation growth in 2021. This boom in wind energy offers significant business opportunities. European-based businesses currently lead this charge but Chinese businesses are gathering pace in terms of innovation and business growth. This isn't fringe activity anymore. This is the heart of new business and we can either watch it happen or we can get involved.

Designing, engineering, building, siting and managing these things creates jobs. They create jobs in disciplines that are transferable between old industry and these new industries. Other renewable sources include the following.

Geothermal energy

Geothermal energy is derived from the natural heat of the earth.

It is the thermal energy contained in the rock and fluid that fills the fractures and pores within the rock of the earth's crust.

Geothermal resources are reservoirs of hot water that exist at different temperatures and depths below the Earth's surface. They exist in both high enthalpy (volcanoes, geysers) and low enthalpy forms (heat stored in rocks in the Earth's crust). Most heating and cooling applications need low enthalpy heat. Geothermal energy has two primary applications: heating/cooling and electricity generation. A coiled heat exchanger is dropped into the drilled hole and water runs through this pulling the heat out. This heat can then be used directly to provide heat for spaces or generate steam that is used to produce electricity. When used for heating and cooling ground source heat pumps use 75 per cent less energy than traditional heating and cooling systems.

Trials run by the Eden Project are returning water in excess of 186°C from around 5,000 metres deep. If we look at the heat stored in the top 10,000 metres of the earth it has been estimated to contain 50,000 times more than all the oil and gas reserves combined.

The International Renewable Energy Agency has reported that 14,438 MW of geothermal power was online worldwide at the end of 2020, generating 94,949 GWh of electricity.[9]

Hydro power

Hydro power is another renewable energy source that has potential. According to the International Energy Agency, hydro power accounted for 17 per cent of global electricity generation in 2020.[10] This form of renewable energy is particularly well-developed in countries like China, Brazil and Canada, where large hydro power projects have been developed. However, the growth of hydro power has been hindered by concerns about its environmental impact, particularly on aquatic ecosystems, and these are real concerns that will keep this one pegged back for some time.

What does all this mean?

We have seen a steady decline in the amount of carbon emitted per kWh. In the UK this has been quite dramatic with DEFRA (the UK's Department for Environment, Food and Rural Affairs) mapping this decline. In the UK in 2013 the carbon intensity per kWh of electricity was 452 g CO_2e/kWh and in 2022 it was just 193 g. I track this weekly and some days it can be as low 120 g. This is predominantly due to renewables with just a dash (10.8 per cent as I type this) of French nuclear power and some of our own.

But we have also become more efficient. We use 12 per cent less energy per household and industry has shrunk its energy footprint (admittedly through the loss of heavy industry) by 60 per cent since 1970.[11]

2 Plastic pollution

Plastic pollution is one of the most visible environmental issues. Every year, millions of tonnes of plastic waste end up in our oceans, rivers and landfills, causing significant harm to wildlife, ecosystems and human health. In terms of the oceans around 90 per cent of this plastic comes from just 10 rivers.[12] Eight of these are in Asia and two in Africa. This is as much a failure of systems as it is materials.

However, over the past few years, there has been a growing awareness of the problem, and efforts are being made to address it at various levels. Governments, non-governmental organizations, businesses and individuals are all playing a role in tackling plastic pollution. These are some of the ways of addressing the issue:

Policies and regulations: Governments around the world are implementing policies and regulations to reduce plastic waste. Many countries have banned or restricted single-use plastic items such as bags, straws and utensils. In the European Union the ban on single-use plastics has been in force since 2021. These policies are aimed at reducing the amount of plastics entering the natural world and focus on the items people are thought to litter the most. Whether you are a user of products and packaging or a manufacturer this will have an impact upon your business.

Circular economy: Recovery and reprocessing is a way many countries have enhanced their recycling programmes. This has been particularly important in the light of China's decision to stop accepting plastic for recycling from overseas. Businesses are increasingly using recycled plastic in their packaging and products and this creates a demand which increases the value of waste plastic. This will have a direct impact on you if you manufacture products or packaging from plastic and it will also impact your recycling and waste disposal costs.

Innovations in alternatives: This is about finding an alternative to plastic. Biodegradable and compostable plastics made from plant-based materials, such as corn starch or sugarcane, are increasingly popular. These materials are supposed to break down naturally in the environment, reducing the amount of plastic waste that ends up in landfills or the ocean. However, there are concerns about the cost and efficiency of producing these alternatives on a large scale and real-life trials reveal that they don't always break down. If they find their way into plastic recycling streams they contaminate a vast amount of material.

Education and awareness: Raising awareness about the problem of plastic pollution is crucial in changing attitudes and behaviour. Plastic doesn't put itself into the natural environment. People do that. Human behaviour and systems failure are the root cause of plastic pollution.

Introducing plastic taxes: Taxation on plastic bags at the point of use has been introduced in a number of countries. Initially plastic bag use falls (it is important to remember, however, that the carbon impact of paper bags is higher and the number of possible re-uses tends to be lower). Importantly, though, the introduction of heavier tax-free bags for life in the UK has resulted in a greater weight of plastic than was saved in single-use bags being used in bags-for-life annually.

Clean-up efforts: Finally, clean-up efforts are reducing the amount of plastic waste in the environment. Many organizations, such as The Ocean Cleanup, are working to remove plastic from the oceans. Clean-up efforts also involve local communities, such as beach clean-ups, to remove plastic waste from coastal areas. However, the best option is to not put the plastic in the wrong place initially.

3 The decline of the internal combustion engine and the rise of EVs

The world has seen a surge in the increase of electric vehicles (EVs). Initially kick-started by Tesla, now every major automotive manufacturer is accelerating the development and launch of new EV models. The key to Tesla's success was not its cars – they're pretty good, but the real thing that needed to be sold was reassurance. Tesla's charging network is key. I've alluded to it previously – we need better systems.

As a business owner or leader you will have noticed the significant tax advantages in place to shift your fleet from fossil-fuel-based to electric. This is particularly generous for owners of limited companies and has stimulated a huge spike in sales. Remember, it's also a really good thing for the planet as we will see in a few pages time.

Changing the way mobility is powered isn't enough. The environmental and social impacts of the car are greater than the fuel used, however in the EU passenger cars and light goods vehicles are responsible for between 5 and 12 per cent of total greenhouse gas emissions[13] and in the United States transport generally is responsible for 27 per cent of greenhouse gas emissions.[14] According to a report by Bloomberg New Energy Finance,[15] the global sales of EVs increased from 1.1 million units in 2017 to 2.1 million units in 2019, showing a growth rate of 90 per cent over two years. In 2020, despite the Covid-19 pandemic, global EV sales increased by a further 43 per cent to 3.2 million units.

Based on these trends, it is expected that the sales of EVs will continue to grow in the coming years. According to the report the global EV market share is expected to reach 10 per cent of total vehicle sales by 2025 and 28 per cent by 2030. EV sales are expected to represent 58 per cent of global passenger vehicle sales by 2040. The International Energy Agency predicts that by 2030, there will be around 145 million electric cars on the road, up from 11 million in 2020. General Motors has announced that it plans to produce only EVs by 2035, while Volkswagen plans to sell 1 million EVs per year by 2025.

Despite the rapid rise in EV adoption, road transport is still not on track for carbon neutrality by 2050. Simply changing out the drivetrain of vehicles may not be the most efficient way to deliver net zero, and a full range of solutions – including more public transit, and active transport options – will be needed. Aggressive action from policy makers and systems designers will be required, especially in cities to help enable people to get to work safely and with less impact. Other challenges exist for business in terms of getting goods delivered to customers. This is especially the case with heavier vehicles, where both batteries and hydrogen fuel cells are vying for a place in the market.

I know what you're thinking. You've read that EVs are more damaging than internal combustion engine (ICE) cars. Well, there is a significant amount of research here. Here's an overview of the major life cycle analysis (LCA) studies that have compared electric cars and ICE cars:

1 'Environmental challenges through the life cycle of battery electric vehicles' (2023)[16]: This study identifies the fact that battery electric vehicles (BEVs) have significantly lower lifetime carbon impact despite a higher manufacturing impact than ICE vehicles. It identifies a 60 per cent reduction in lifetime carbon impact (including manufacturing) of the BEV over ICE in average European driving conditions. Similarly the study 'Comparative environmental life cycle assessment of conventional vehicles with different fuel options, plug-in hybrid and electric vehicles for a sustainable transportation system in Brazil' (2018)[17] analysed 43 LCA studies of EVs and ICE cars and found that EVs had lower life cycle greenhouse gas emissions compared to ICE cars. The study also found that the manufacturing phase of EVs had higher environmental impacts, but the operational and end-of-life phases had lower impacts compared to ICE cars.

2 A further study[18] looked in more depth at different country scenarios taking into account electricity supply impacts and driving conditions. It found that emissions over the lifetime of average medium-size BEVs registered today are already lower than comparable gasoline cars by 66–69 per cent in Europe, 60–68 per cent in the United States, 37–45 per cent in China and 19–34 per cent in India. Additionally, as the electricity mix continues to decarbonize, the life cycle emissions gap between BEVs

and gasoline vehicles increases substantially when considering medium-size cars projected to be registered in 2030.

3 A study looking at a similar LCA but also considering scenarios where high-impact raw materials are used found that the lifetime impacts of BEVs were a little under 20 tonnes of CO_2e compared to ICE vehicles at an average of 41 tonnes CO_2e.[19] Higher-impact raw materials made a tiny difference to the BEV total pushing it up to 21 tonnes.

4 'A review of the life cycle assessment of electric vehicles: Considering the influence of batteries' (2022)[20]: This study reviewed 29 LCA studies of hybrid and electric vehicles and found that EVs had lower life cycle environmental impacts compared to ICE cars, primarily due to the lower greenhouse gas emissions during the operational phase.

5 'Measuring life-cycle carbon emissions of private transportation in urban and rural settings' (2023)[21]: This study compared the life cycle greenhouse gas emissions of EVs and ICE cars in Colombia. The study found that EVs had lower life cycle greenhouse gas emissions compared to ICE cars, primarily due to the lower emissions during the operational phase.

There are many more, all coming to the same conclusion that EVs have lower life cycle environmental impacts compared to ICE cars, due in particular to lower greenhouse gas emissions during the operational phase.

The challenge with BEVs is the battery technology and the extraction of the raw materials required to manufacture the batteries.

According to a report by the World Bank, the demand for critical metals, such as lithium, cobalt, nickel and manganese, is expected to increase significantly with the growth of the EV market.

However, it's important to note that there are various estimates of future demand for raw materials for EV batteries, and they can vary significantly depending on assumptions and methodologies. A report by BloombergNEF[22] suggests that there will be sufficient supplies of lithium, cobalt and nickel to meet the demand for EV batteries until 2030. However, there are still concerns that supply of these materials could create a bottleneck and slow adoption of EV technology.[23]

In terms of capacity, the production of raw materials for EV batteries is also expected to increase significantly in the coming years. BloombergNEF estimates that the production capacity of lithium-ion batteries will increase from 455 GWh in 2020 to 1,200 GWh in 2025, and 4,000 GWh in 2030. This represents a more than eight-fold increase in capacity in just a decade.

The other question often posed is whether we have the electricity capacity to power a transition to BEVs. The National Renewable Energy Laboratory (NREL) in the United States estimated that if all light-duty vehicles in the country were replaced with EVs, it would result in an increase in electricity demand of around 25 per cent.[24] Similar estimates apply to the EU.

While there are concerns about the availability of raw materials for EV batteries, there are also efforts underway to increase production capacity and develop alternative battery technologies that require fewer or different raw materials. There are some promising signs here. I won't go into too much detail but these are the most promising technologies:

- **Carbon nanotube electrodes:** This is a technology which improves current batteries by using vertically aligned carbon nanotubes. In tests these have boosted battery power by as much as tenfold. Best of all, they can be charged to 80 per cent in just five minutes. This technology will be available in the short term.[25]
- **Cobalt-free batteries:** Researchers at the University of Texas have developed Cobalt-free batteries. Not only does this reduce supply-chain risk and avoid resource availability issues it has also been shown to hold enough charge for 500 miles range.[26]
- **Sea-water batteries:** This technology is attracting significant interest at the moment given the abundance of sea water. They are made from sodium-sulphur (a type of salt readily extracted from sea water) and research at the University of Sydney indicates that these batteries dramatically reduce costs whilst providing up to four times the storage capacity of lithium.[27] This technology will also support the acceleration of renewables by allowing more cost-efficient and less impactful energy storage.

It is likely that governmental tax incentives to aid the transition to EVs will taper off. But a simple comparison of running costs makes a strong enough business case. The cost per mile driven is around half that of fossil fuelled cars (assuming they are predominantly charged at home or at the workplace and taking into account the historic electricity price rises of 2021/22). Furthermore, the servicing costs are less than half that of an ICE vehicle. As we have already seen the environmental impact is significantly less than ICE vehicles. Twinned with solar power systems the costs of EVs are a fraction of ICE vehicles.

4 The sustainability of cities and the built environment

The buildings in which we grow our businesses and our lives have significant embedded impact and even larger impact in their running and maintenance. From an environmental perspective building design has improved considerably over the last decade. The most notable enhancements are:

- Buildings are designed to be more energy efficient, lowering the amount of energy used for heating, cooling and lighting. A combination of low energy materials in the build, re-processing materials and using them again, and a move to modern methods of construction (MMC) has reduced environmental impact in a number of ways including significant waste reduction through off-site manufacture and industrial assembly, the use of timber and other materials to replace brick and concrete, the use of brick-slips (a thinner layer of bricks covering a steel or wooden-framed structure), and less time onsite reduces disruption of flora and fauna.
- Water efficiency in building construction has been enhanced for both financial and environmental reasons.

This is in large part due to the replacement of the wet trades and brick construction with steel structures and MMC.

- Using lower carbon materials has also been accelerated in order both to reduce costs and move to meet the net zero goal. This has included the use of recycled and re-purposed materials, designing and building for a second and third life, and moving towards low-carbon concrete. The use of low-carbon concrete has increased by 64 per cent globally between 2017 and 2019 and has a stretching net zero timeline.[28]

- In terms of design there has been an increased focus on incorporating nature into building design using bio-philic design principles. This includes adding green roofs, living walls and natural lighting. Biophilic design has been shown to improve occupant well-being and productivity while also reducing energy consumption by mimicking natural systems and structures, connect-ing people more closely with nature and building in natural landscape features. According to a study pub-lished in the *Journal of Experimental Psychology Ap-plied*,[29] offices with natural elements had a 15 per cent higher well-being score than those without.

- There has been considerable growth in the use of build-ing automation systems (BAS) in business spaces. The integration of BAS has enabled buildings to be more ef-ficient in their operations. BAS allows for the monitor-ing and control of various building systems, including heating, ventilation and lighting, to optimize energy use. According to a report by Navigant Research, the global market for BAS is expected to grow by 10.8 per cent annually through 2027.[30]

5 Regenerative agriculture

Food is often described as medicine. We can eat our way healthy. But food is also medicine for the planet. Over the last 100 years we have developed a form of agriculture that has damaged the earth's ability to grow food, that has damaged biodiversity, increased the risk of flooding and reduced the nutritional value of the food we grow. Monocultures, industrial animal farming, excessive use of pesticides and herbicides, and the industrialization of farming fed us but on the way caused significant damage. Changing agricultural models is urgent and the rise of the concept of regenerative agriculture offers hope. Applied widely, it will increase soil carbon content, increase the ability of the soil to hold water and will offer carbon sequestration opportunities.

Regenerative agriculture is an approach that focuses on improving the health of the soil, which in turn leads to and is supported by more productive and sustainable farming practices. It involves using techniques that increase biodiversity, promote healthy soil and reduce the use of synthetic fertilizers and pesticides.

There is a significant body of literature on the subject but to summarize the benefits:

Improved soil health

The most significant benefit (or at least the most desired benefits) of regenerative agriculture is improved soil health. By focusing on building healthy soil, farmers can increase the fertility of their land, reduce erosion and improve water retention. This leads to higher crop yields, profitability and better overall plant health. In addition, healthy soil can sequester carbon from the atmosphere, reducing greenhouse gas emissions and mitigating the effects of climate change.

Increased biodiversity

By using techniques such as crop rotation, cover cropping and intercropping, farmers can create a more diverse ecosystem on their land. This can lead to a greater variety of plants and animals, which can in turn help to control pests and diseases and promote a healthier ecosystem. As we begin to embrace the concept of net gain, and as net gain strategies become a legal requirement and we inevitably need to net gain offset, there will be significant opportunities for business diversification and enhanced profitability. We are all nature companies now. If you use raw materials that are grown or pulled from the ground enhancing biodiversity is central to your environmental and business strategies.

Reduced dependence on synthetic inputs

Regenerative agriculture focuses on reducing the use of synthetic inputs such as fertilizers and pesticides. Instead, farmers use natural methods such as composting, crop rotation and biological pest control. This not only reduces the environmental impact of agriculture but can increase sustainable profits.

Improved economic outcomes

Regenerative agriculture has been shown to improve economic outcomes for farmers. By improving soil health and reducing the need for synthetic inputs, farmers can increase crop yields and reduce costs. Regenerative agriculture can also create new income streams for farmers through practices such as agroforestry and rotational grazing. Add in the opportunity to enter the carbon sequestration market and there are significant opportunities for business here.

Improved community health

Regenerative agriculture can also have a positive impact on community health. By reducing the use of synthetic inputs, farmers can reduce the amount of harmful chemicals in the environment. Regenerative agriculture can create new opportunities for local food production and distribution, leading to improved access to fresh, healthy food for local communities.

Increased resilience to climate change

Finally, regenerative agriculture can increase resilience to climate change. By improving soil health and increasing biodiversity, farmers can create more resilient ecosystems that are better able to withstand extreme weather events such as droughts and floods and mitigate the effects of climate change.[31]

Increasingly, consumers demand more environmentally benign food and drink. Consumers may not be aware of the words 'regenerative agriculture' (only 19 per cent of respondents to a recent US survey had heard of the practice)[32] but there is an increasing majority of younger consumers wanting to eat food that has less environmental impact.[33] The potential to meet this demand while simultaneously improving soil and sequestering carbon is a perfect business opportunity. There is profit to be made by doing good and doing business for good.

6 Environmental education

Let's stay with the consumer for a minute. As a result of becoming more aware – as result of becoming better educated about sustainability and the way that products are made and sold – we are changing what we want from businesses. There is a hunger for increased environmental education.

While environmental education at secondary and tertiary levels is becoming more prevalent, we have also seen the incorporation of hands-on learning into formal education and into business. This allows learners to understand environmental concepts by engaging in activities that relate to them, the work they do and your business. Much of this has been driven by legislation and in particular the advent of producer responsibility legislation which asks complex and challenging questions about the sustainability of products and processes but also about the fundamentals of business plans and business processes. This is good, it brings issues to life that can otherwise sometimes feel a little academic or esoteric. Adding real-world dimensions and applications triggers interest in a way that didactic teaching can't.

We have also witnessed a shift to a more interdisciplinary approach. Environmental education has evolved to encompass a wider range of topics, incorporating subjects like social studies, and economics. This approach helps employees and learners to understand the interconnectedness of environmental issues with other fields and across their business.

Sustainability sits at the heart of many subjects and disciplines. Half the problems that we have are because of seeing it as a separate thing. Therefore, taking a more interdisciplinary approach and embedding it into all aspects of your business and training means that it becomes everyone's job. My favourite example of this is in the UK with Marks & Spencer's Plan A programme. In the late 1990s the organization was falling a good way behind the competition in terms of sustainability. I was working in this sector at that time and to describe the organization as a laggard would be about right. Then they changed. Mike Barry arrived as Head of Sustainable Business and kick-started a programme of activity that shifted them from laggard to leader. I won't go into detail as what to Plan A was, but one element ensured it entered the company culture and changed that culture. This is the fact that every product sold had to have a Plan A attribute. This wasn't prescribed narrowly; indeed, it was left wonderfully open, but it ensured that every buyer, merchandizer and strategist had sustainability on their agenda. Making it real and putting it into an interdisciplinary space ensured it was more than marketing.

The need for critical and creative thinking is widespread across many businesses and roles. This is a good thing as it facilitates innovation and creativity. Those businesses that struggle and fail have often lost the ability to think creatively and to be critically constructive. Think Quibi, Yahoo, Kodak, ToysRUs, Blockbuster and Borders. All experienced difficult trading environments and shifting technology but while others grew these businesses failed to think critically and innovate. Thankfully environmental education has shifted from memorization of facts to an emphasis on critical thinking. This approach allows employees to analyse, experiment and develop their own conclusions and solutions to environmental problems.

More broadly environmental education and education in general has been boosted by technology. Technology has allowed environmental education to reach a larger audience. Virtual and online learning tools have made it easier for learners to access environmental education resources and information. Clearly there is a significant 'watch out' here as there is also a risk of being educated by misinformation. There is a real risk of teaching people the wrong things, of championing opinion over science, and in taking us closer to rather than further from environmental problems, so be incredibly careful to check the credentials of the people teaching or leading learning. As a business owner or leader you could pull together a series of resources and make them available for the team. Alternatively talk to your trade association and see what education services they offer.

7 The changing consumer

The consumer is changing their aspirations and their behaviour. This offers significant opportunities for businesses.

These needs are aligned with beliefs that aren't restricted to consuming more. They are often aligned with doing better.

Some years ago I was asked by a large food company to help them understand changing consumer preferences around sweetness. They had identified a small (it was actually about 25 per cent) proportion of their consumers who expressed a preference for less-sweet foods. The problem was that this company made sweet foods. They were beginning to get worried as they had applied the usual consumer understanding lenses and asked me to help work out who these people were.

They weren't all in one convenient category: not all women in their 20s, not all college-educated women in their 30s, not all men in their 40s who read *The Times*, not all ABC1s. None of the traditional ways of understanding the consumer was helping. We looked at this and interviewed over 100 consumers, tracked 20 of them for a week and got them to record what they consumed and why. We developed a new model based on consumer beliefs, aspirations and behaviours. From here we developed a series of archetypes to help understand these new behaviours.

We were seeing a series of new beliefs based around the broad areas of sustainability, health, mental well-being and social progression. These beliefs were manifest in many different ways but we attempted to map them and then align with aspirations and then the behaviours that arise from those aspirations.

The tiering looked like this:

- First – Macro beliefs
- Second – Micro beliefs

- Third – Aspirations
- Fourth – Behaviours

What does this look like? Let's work through the less-sweet example.

First – Macro beliefs

In the case of sweetness, the core macro beliefs that we identified were health and sustainability. Health was seen in a number of ways and it is exceptionally complex. Some people see weight and size as a totem for health. While not true it is a widely held belief. Health was also concerned with longevity and aging well, and seen as avoiding complex ingredients. There was some understanding of holistic health that also considered gut health and the gut–brain link. There was an additional perception regarding sweetness achieved through artificial means. These artificial sweeteners were perceived by around half of respondents as unnatural and bad for planet and people. Sustainability in terms of sweetness focused on the type of sugar with beet being seen as more sustainable than cane sugar. Artificial sweeteners were again generally seen as unsustainable. Any large producer of products (food or non-food) were seen as unsustainable. This last one is a great bridge into the next tier – micro beliefs.

Second – Micro beliefs

Our macro beliefs are a general direction that we would like society to move in and one that we can align ourselves to. However, the micro beliefs dig down into specifics, they may also contradict another person's micro beliefs.

What do I mean here? Well, let's take sustainability as our core belief. One macro belief may well focus on ocean health and plastic pollution. That's laudable. However, as we have seen, the biggest threat to ocean health is climate change and a shift to glass beverage containers will increase the threat of climate change. Therefore, there is a potential conflict between two micro beliefs that try and meet the same macro belief. There are plenty of other examples: hydrogen-powered cars versus electric cars, veganism versus regenerative agriculture. These micro beliefs can be massively influenced by personal experience, culture and political ideology.

Examples of micro beliefs in the case of sweetness (and aligning to the macro beliefs of sustainability and health) include: the view that 'chemicals' are bad and therefore clean-eating is the way forward; the view that sugar is bad for health generally and metabolic health in particular; the view that small companies and brands are better and have more interest in supporting health and sustainability so are better trusted (there is little evidence for this in reality); the view that less-sweet products are better for gut health; the view that smaller companies take greater care of the environment and their people; the view that curiosity for different flavours will lead away from sweetness. The list goes on but there are enough here to give you an idea of how these beliefs work together.

Third – Aspirations

These are focused on the type of world we want to live in, the type of person we want to be or (at worst) the type of person we want people to think we are. What? What is Shayler saying? Well, it's simple. In a world where projection matters as much as reality, where it didn't happen unless you Instagrammed it, where we explain who we are by what we buy rather than what we think and say, our environmental posturing is becoming endemic. We project our values even if we don't live them.

These aspirations form our behaviours and in this case could include: a view that small companies are better for me and the planet; a view that adopting health-focused and sustainable behaviour is in some way 'cool'; a view that hunting out unusual flavours and ingredients is desirable and ahead of the curve as well as avoiding sweetness.

Fourth – Behaviours

This is where we really see change (or not). What do these shifts in belief systems actually mean? What do people do with their beliefs? Do they follow through into behaviour? There is a phenomenon known as the value–action gap: numerous studies have shown that while many people express concern about environmental issues, such as climate change, pollution and deforestation, their actual behaviour often does not reflect that concern. For example, people may say they support renewable energy sources, but still rely heavily on fossil fuels in their daily lives.

There are a number of reasons why this gap exists. One reason is that people may not always have access to or be aware of environmentally preferential options. It could be that the individual has many values and prioritizes one over another. These may not be purposeful values; they may simply be value, cost or convenience. There is also a fear of dilution. As an individual or a single business it is easy to feel overwhelmed by the scale of the challenge and this potentially results in the thought (or fear) that small actions do not make any or a significant difference in the face of large-scale environmental problems. This can lead to a sense of hopelessness and apathy, which can further contribute to the value–action gap.

Let's return to our example of those consumers expressing a preference for less-sweet food and drinks. Our study identified modified behaviour in the majority of consumers. What did they do? Some sought out simpler food and drink with fewer ingredients (interestingly these could still contain sugar or sweeteners, they seemed to conflate less-sweet with 'clean label'); some simply avoided sugars and sweeteners but made no other changes; some avoided sweetness and tried to persuade others to do the same, they became evangelical about things; some began to seek out other flavours, new flavours to take over from sweetness (umami, acidity, that kind of thing); some aligned less-sweet with start-up brands as these brands like to fight against something and health is a great place to do this; and some just cut down. All of these offer significant business opportunities to those companies engaged positively with the consumer.

The way the consumer (your customer) behaves is changing. We are seeing the growth of blended consumption (matching a Gucci suit with a pair of rubber Birkenstocks) but this isn't about price; these consumers are buying from companies that they share one belief with (Gucci – high fashion, Birkenstock – foot health and vegan). Therefore understanding the beliefs of your customers is the key to growing a business and doing so sustainably.

8 A rise in environmental activism

It won't have escaped your attention that there has been a significant rise in environmental activism since 2018. How does this impact business? How has this climate of activism emerged?

Things started with the youth-led climate strikes: in 2018, a 15-year-old Swedish activist named Greta Thunberg started skipping school to protest outside parliament, demanding action on climate change. Her actions inspired a global movement of young people, who organized massive strikes and protests demanding that governments take action. These protests have taken place in cities all over the world and have involved millions of young people. These are our kids, your kids. When your kids ask you to change the way you make money you have to listen.

In recent years, there has been a significant increase in the number of protests against new fossil fuel infrastructure projects, such as pipelines and oil rigs. The Standing Rock Sioux Tribe led a protest against the Dakota Access Pipeline in 2016, which drew international attention and support from environmental activists around the world.

And there are new forms of activism and new organizations. In 2018, a new environmental activist group called Extinction Rebellion (XR) was formed in the United Kingdom. XR's main goal is to force governments to take action on the climate crisis by using non-violent direct action, such as protests and civil disobedience. XR has organized large-scale protests in cities around the world, including London, New York and Sydney. They have attracted widespread support including significant celebrity endorsement.[34]

In 2021 and 2022, a group called Insulate Britain caused havoc in the United Kingdom. They are campaigning for the government to take immediate action to insulate all homes and buildings in the country. The aim of the group is to reduce carbon emissions and tackle the climate crisis by improving energy efficiency. The group has been staging protests and blockades on major roads across the UK, with the intention of causing disruption to draw attention to their cause. The protests have been controversial and have led to arrests and criticism from some members of the public who have been inconvenienced by the blockades. Insulate Britain argued that the UK government is not doing enough to tackle the climate crisis, and that insulating buildings is a simple and cost-effective solution that would create jobs and save people money on energy bills. This would also stimulate the economy and give rise to a myriad of green business opportunities.

Then we see a more focused approach towards the financial world with calls for divestment in investment in fossil fuels. Given the fact that return on investment into renewables is significantly more lucrative it seems odd that there is still any major investment in the fossil fuel sector. However, a study published in 2020 by the Institute for Energy Economics and Financial Analysis (IEEFA)[35] found that the world's 100 largest public pension funds collectively held over $1.4 trillion in fossil fuel investments, representing roughly 4.2 per cent of their total assets under management. However, the study also noted that some funds, particularly those in Europe, had significantly reduced their exposure to fossil fuels in recent years. In some cases, pension funds have also faced pressure from their members and other stakeholders to divest.

There are many ways to protest and many forms of activism. This may all seem a long way from business but it cuts to the heart of what kind of economy will be acceptable in the future and how we make money by putting things right.

9 TV production as activism

The growth of streaming services and the explosion of independent production has resulted in an increase in documentaries about environmental issues. These documentaries aim to raise awareness about the impact of human activity on the environment and highlight the need for action.

Many of these documentaries have become popular and have been widely viewed. Some of the most well-known documentaries on environmental issues include *An Inconvenient Truth*, *Chasing Ice*, *Cowspiracy*, *The True Cost*, *A Plastic Ocean*, *Seaspiracy* and *Gamechangers*.

These documentaries cover a wide range of issues, such as climate change, deforestation, pollution and the impact of industrial agriculture. They use powerful images and compelling storytelling to engage viewers and inspire them to take action.

Activism is closely allied to education. As we become more exposed to environmental education it is likely that we become more engaged in wanting to solve problems and to raise awareness.

It is important to remember, however, that all environmental activism offers both a threat and a significant opportunity for business. Firstly the disruption of closing down city centres and roads leads to problems with logistics and disruption of business as usual, which is of course the aim of these protests. Secondly, however, there is an associated suite of opportunities here. If we go back to the research on belief-driven consumers from Gartner, over half of consumers define themselves this way and two-thirds of that number will avoid businesses that fail to take a position on issues that the public feel they should engage with. There is an appetite to do business with companies that align with greater purpose. But over-claiming any activity here pushes consumers' scepticism buttons and could produce a backlash. The real opportunity here is gaining an understanding of the trajectory and desires of the public. How can you tap into this changed appetite for better and develop products and services that align with these?

10 Brand authenticity

All of these changes in consumer behaviour are having an impact on consumer-facing businesses as they try and find a brand position that is honest and reflects consumer beliefs. This is a narrow gap in which to work and brands increasingly seek to find an authentic voice. Sometimes they need to take a strong position on a social issue, other times they need look at the reason they started and rediscover their original purpose.

The Japanese typewriter and sewing machine company Brother wanted to work with me on their sustainability purpose. We dug deep into archive and history, we looked at what people thought of the products and we went and watched companies use the machines. We found that in all the edgy start-ups and artisan makers of clothing, there was a Brother machine upon which the work was done. These were up to 60 years old. The longevity was incredible. We came up with the line 'Brother, the maker's maker' and were able to talk honestly about the durability of the machines.

I have worked with Nike two or three times but I wasn't responsible for their bravest stance. In 2016, NFL quarterback Colin Kaepernick began protesting police brutality and racial injustice by kneeling during the national anthem before games. The protest sparked a national controversy, with some people supporting Kaepernick's message and others criticizing the perceived disrespect for the American flag and military.

Nike, one of Kaepernick's sponsors, faced pressure from both sides of the debate. In 2018, the company featured Kaepernick in a new ad campaign with the tagline 'Believe in something. Even if it means sacrificing everything.' The campaign received both praise and criticism, with some people calling for a boycott of Nike products.

Despite the backlash, Nike's sales reportedly increased after the campaign. Kaepernick also became a prominent social justice activist and philanthropist, launching the Know Your Rights Camp to provide resources and education to disadvantaged communities.

The key here is to find genuineness to hang your authenticity on. You can't go inventing stuff. That's just lying. I once ran a workshop on authentic marketing for 50 or so marketeers. When I had finished one of the attendees raised his hand and said 'So what you are saying is that we should, as an industry, stop lying?'

Yes, yes, that's exactly what I am saying. Stop lying. Don't tell me you're funny, make me laugh. Twinned with my mantra of 'it's not sufficient to do things better, we must do better things' and we have a good starting point to develop brand authenticity and begin to grow and build trust. Trust is everything. Once you have the customer's trust do not lose it.

Trusting in brand authenticity has become increasingly important for consumers, particularly for those generations who place a premium on transparency and ethical business practices. The following are a number of brands that have taken steps to be more authentic in recent years.

Patagonia has made sustainability and ethical practices a core part of its brand. The company has been transparent about its supply chain and has taken steps to reduce its environmental impact. When their supply chain for wool was found to include the mistreatment of animals they stood up and came clean about it, then put it right. The company has taken a stand on political and social issues, such as climate change and protecting public lands. This commitment to sustainability and social responsibility has helped the brand resonate with consumers who value authenticity and who have beliefs based around sustainability.

Dove is a personal care brand owned by Unilever. Dove has been recognized for its campaigns that celebrate diversity and challenge beauty standards. Its 'Real Beauty' campaign has been lauded for promoting body positivity and inclusivity. The brand has also been transparent about its commitment to sustainability, and has taken steps to reduce its environmental impact.

REI is an American specialty outdoor retailer who has made authenticity a core part of its brand. The company has a strong commitment to sustainability and ethical business practices and has been transparent about its supply chain and the impact of its products. REI has taken steps to promote outdoor recreation and conservation and has been involved in advocacy efforts to protect public lands.

More companies recognize the importance of transparency, ethical practices and social responsibility in building a strong and loyal customer base. It can go horribly wrong when the thing you are trying to champion wasn't built into your DNA in the first place. Budweiser found this in April 2023 when they launched a programme of awareness around trans rights. Within hours there were boycotts of the product and examples of it being destroyed in-store. Fundamentally they were doing a good thing with the campaign but they hadn't factored in the reality that a proportion of their core consumer did not share the same beliefs. Furthermore, to be authentic you need to have been engaged in this stuff for a while. Ben & Jerry's (the ice cream brand owned by Unilever) have been activists for decades, and their customers get this stuff, therefore they have every right to take a stand and most importantly their customers expect it.

But what if you sell business-to-business rather than business-to-consumer? The same applies. Businesses need to trust their suppliers, but more than that they need to help communicate sustainability and authenticity from wherever they are in the supply chain to the end consumer.

Brand authenticity needs to start at the heart of the business, it isn't marketing. It is storytelling and truth-telling. You can't suddenly become a brand activist, you need to have stood for something bigger than you for a while or enter this arena gently and with respect.

CHAPTER SIX

How do we do good and still turn a profit?

In this chapter I turn to look at how to build a better business, one that does good and one that ultimately will allow you to grow a regenerative business. This is a big section of the book and we dig into the science and methods to transform your business and begin to redress the problems we have created. For that we need better business.

But what does 'better' mean?

We know business has to change, has to be better. But what does this mean? Business originally had a legal responsibility to generate and distribute profits to its shareholders. But nothing else. Clearly this wasn't good enough and over the decades legislation has been implemented to protect people and planet. This is great. But it is really about doing 'less bad'. I'm firmly of the opinion that business has created most of the world's problems, but it's the only thing that can solve them. But more than that, the power of business to do social good, to create and redistribute wealth, is untapped. There are some really interesting trends becoming apparent in terms of new models of ownership: community-owned businesses, employee-owned businesses, cooperatives and not-for-profits. These are amazing and should be welcomed, but a 'standard' business can do better too.

I have been working with business for over 30 years. I have advised thousands of businesses. I can honestly say that in all that time and in all those businesses I have only met around a dozen people who wanted to do harm, or who saw profit at all costs as their aim. I am acutely aware that this is a self-selecting sample. Those people who want advice on sustainability are perhaps less likely to be heartless than those who don't. But the interesting point here is that the reasons people ask me for advice have changed significantly over this time. When I started my consulting work I was offering free sustainability advice to businesses on behalf of the local authority in Bradford in the UK. This was 1993. Sustainability wasn't widely spoken about in business, and when it was the conversation was related to prosecution over pollution incidents. Therefore, the question I was asked was:

'Mark, can you help keep me out of prison?'

Yep, of course I can, we just need to comply with the environmental regulations and understand why they are there in the first place.

We were in difficult financial times at this point. We were in the long tail of the 1990 recession and therefore cost savings were high on the agenda. Therefore, the next question I'd be asked was:

'Mark, can you help keep me lean?'

Yep, of course I can. Sustainability mainly reduces costs. Investing in efficient and lean processes that embrace recyclate as a cheaper feedstock, using efficient machinery that may cost more but will pay back in the medium term, removing waste, re-using resources, getting more product or utility from the same resources and time are all environmentally sensible and will all increase profitability.

My mantra is:

If sustainability is costing you money then you're doing it wrong.

I appreciate that there are step-change investments such as new packaging or capital equipment investments, but the payback should be fast. I've saved my clients in excess of $160 million, annually, through sustainability initiatives. Yes, I wish I was on a percentage payment too.

Then the discipline of brand and reputation management became important. Today many companies' brand assets are worth more than their physical assets. But back in the 1990s this was an emerging discipline. Brands were protected by keeping them out of the press. Hence the next question I was asked a lot was...

'Mark, can you keep me out of the papers?'

Yep, I can. The first step is to not break any laws (see above), then to cause no nuisance.

I've a story here. I worked with a company who made fish food. Fish food is made from dead fish. It is mixed with other materials and then cooked in very thin sheets. It's a very odorous process and the factory had a tall chimney with the relevant 'scrubbers' (technologies to remove smells and other pollutants). But although the technology removed any issues regarding environmental consents it wasn't sufficient to remove all the odours and there were many complaints. To counter this the company paid an employee to drive around the area after his shift inside the factory. His task was to sniff the air and identify whether or not there was a smell issue. The problem was that he was completely desensitized to the smell of fish food having worked in the factory for eight hours a day for 20 years. We solved the problem by upgrading the technology and then pulling together a team of residents who would mark the odour at certain times of the day with a score out of 10 and then call in the number. This allowed the company to understand their nuisance impact and to cross-reference it with weather conditions, the type of product being made that day and the production schedule.

We then moved into an era of risk adversity and control. This is a good thing but led to the question...

'Mark, can you keep me risk-free?'

Now, the answer here is 'yes, I can help'. Understanding your risks extends beyond compliance with the law. The fundamental area of concern here is potential risk to the environment, and this splits into risk to land, air, water and in-use risks. But it's more than that; it embraces supply chain risks (inability to supply), resource scarcity risks, waste treatment risks, consumer demand risks (from an environment perspective) and distribution risks (price and availability of fuel for example). Sustainability is only one element of this but it is an increasingly important element. Having an effective risk register (we will cover this in greater detail later) is essential.

Building on this and a raft of legislation termed the Producer Responsibility Obligations, the issue of buying from a compliant supply chain rather than just a cheap supply chain gave rise to the question...

'Mark, can you keep me supply-chain compliant?'

The End of Life Vehicles legislation, the Waste Electrical and Electronic Equipment Directive, The Restriction of Hazardous Substances Directive and the Registration, Evaluation, Authorisation and Restriction of Chemicals Directive in the UK all brought attention to the need for supply chain transparency and security in terms of compliance. The need to establish reliable supply chain information and records was a shock to many industries.

As a brand you are only as compliant as your most risky supplier.

So I got involved in building toolkits and systems for supply chain assurance.

Then the age of brand hit full stride and the need to impress upon your customers that you cared became really important. This lead to a rash of greenwashing. The question became...

'Mark, can you keep me looking good?'

Now, this was the wrong question. At this stage I'd been working in a (failed) partnership with a branding agency so I understood brand and I already understood storytelling. So I knew that the correct question should have been: 'Mark, can you help us tell our environmental story better?'

Yes, of course. It starts with having a suite of actions. There is a well-used phrase in marketing (and I've seen many friends fall foul of this one): 'never let the truth get in the way of a good story'. But good stories need the truth running through them like the word 'BLACKPOOL' runs through a stick of UK rock. I'll talk you through how the consumer has changed and why they need and deserve the truth a little later in the book, but suffice to say at this stage that you *must* let truth get in the way of the story, actually you need to build the story on truth. For too long many people saw marketing as just persuasive lying. Those days are gone.

Then as the business world woke up to sustainability and it became a rush for the top the noise grew and grew. Everyone was doing something, everyone was 'A B-Corp don't you know'. Here's a joke: How can you tell if someone is B-Corp registered? Don't ask them because they are about to tell you. This isn't necessarily a bad thing but it isn't a good thing either. More on this later too. In a noisy world maybe the quiet ones garner the most attention.

So the question became...

'Mark, can you keep me ahead of my competitors?'

This is a fascinating question. The answer depends on how you want to stay ahead. Marketing noise? Believability? Trust? Reliability? Still here in 20 years?

I can help with most of those. I say this phrase a lot: 'Kindness is a competitive advantage.'

And I believe it.

Being kind is not a weakness, it is a strength. Treat your supply chain, your team and your customers well, treat the environment well, be cooperative with your competitors, be kind to your neighbours. That is how you stay relevant, attract and retain the best talent in the world, and continue to grow.

Moving on naturally from this came the question...

'Mark, can you keep me relevant to my customers?'

This is the current question that I get asked. The truth here is that the way we understand the customer or the consumer is changing. We used to talk about age or gender, or education as a way of categorizing the consumer and therefore as a way of understanding their wants and needs and consequently targeting an offer. The customer is now more informed (mostly), more opinionated and more motivated by their core beliefs. I've shared my model on understanding consumer beliefs earlier in this book. Can I help companies stay relevant? Yes of course. As long as they make a product or deliver a service that is socially progressive, answers a real consumer need and does these things with minimal environmental impact. Easy? I'm going to show you how.

Science matters

We sit at an unusual point in our fight to save the planet (and therefore us). The majority of the public (78 per cent of US consumers according to a recent study by Nielsen IQ) say that a sustainable lifestyle is important to them, and McKinsey identified that 60 per cent of US consumers would pay more for a product with sustainable packaging.[1] This is great news. But the consumer's understanding of science needs some attention.

Current levels of scientific literacy vary greatly among different populations and individuals worldwide. While some countries have made significant efforts to improve science education and promote science literacy, others still struggle with inadequate resources and educational systems. Additionally, the proliferation of misinformation and disinformation on social media has contributed to a lack of understanding and trust in scientific information. It is essential to continue promoting science education and critical thinking skills to ensure that individuals have the knowledge and tools to navigate complex scientific issues.

There is a real risk that concerns about sustainability will be ignored due to low levels of scientific understanding plus misinformation from the 'alt news' providers who attempt to plant seeds of doubt in order to rubbish an argument.

Additionally, green claims are currently a hot topic of debate in every economy. As governments make net zero pledges, businesses are making the same pledges and failing to explain what this means. For example, they are making 'green' packaging claims which fail to recognize the limited and efficient systems the packaging goes into (this means that the 'better' packaging is often worse), and they conflate non-plastic materials with good which is not always the case.

Let's look at two examples.

Example 1: Drinks packaging

This one always garners a significant amount of attention as it is front and centre of people's minds due to the mighty Sir David Attenborough's *Blue Planet 2* Episode 7 which broadcast on the BBC on 10 December 2017. This episode was bookended by two massive issues. One was plastic waste and its impact upon the ocean. That is the bit that everyone can remember. What was the other issue? It was given the same air time as plastic. In my workshops the majority of people I ask do not know what this issue was; they can't remember half of the programme as the other half was so moving. It was climate change, and it is the biggest threat to ocean life.

Why do people remember the plastic issue? It is so very visual. Visual and heart-wrenching. Clearly there should be no place for plastic in the ocean, but the focus of attention on one material serves as a distraction from the most urgent challenges we face which are climate change and collapse of biodiversity (particularly pollenating insects). I'm not saying that we need to ignore the plastic pollution problem, just that we need to get it into perspective. With plastic it's also really easy to blame 'someone else' rather than examine our own behaviours. But is it really the worst environmental option? Let's have a quick and simple look at the subject of drinks packaging.

The main options for a packaged drink are a glass bottle, an aluminium can, a plastic (PET) bottle, a carton-board pack (Tetra, for example), a paper bottle and a pouch.

CARTON-BOARD BACK (FOR EXAMPLE, TETRA)

The first thing packaging has to do is contain and transfer the product safely. Therefore, if we are looking at a carbonated drink the carton-board pack won't cope with the pressure and will barrel, so it is best used for still liquids. Carton-board packs are a lamination of a number of materials. The lining is LDPE (low density polyethylene). This creates a waterproof layer between the drink and the next layer. The next layer is aluminium (not all carton-board packaging has this aluminium layer – it is a UV light blocker and extends shelf-life) and this is 'glued' into the sandwich with another layer of polyethylene on each side. After this is a layer of paperboard/cardboard. This is 'glued' to the aluminium by the aforementioned polyethylene and it is this that creates the structure of the packaging. Print is applied to this layer and then there is another layer of polyethylene as the pack has to deal with condensation and it's not great if the whole thing dissolves from the outside. Then a HDPE (high density polyethylene) closure is fixed into a preformed hole to allow the consumer to use and then reseal the packaging.

We have a complex laminate of materials. This means that it is hard to recycle. Hard but not impossible. The manufacturers have invested heavily in this and are able to either reprocess the packaging into a composite board or split it back down into constituent parts.

What are the advantages of this packaging? First up is tessellation. This describes the way that the packaging can nest inside a bigger box. As the packs are square there is no wasted space in the secondary packaging. Next up is that embedded carbon impact of the pack (this is a measure of the carbon equivalent impact of raw material extraction, processing, conversion and final forming into a package). With such a complex sandwich of materials there are varying estimates as to the carbon intensity. I developed a carbon ready reckoner with the University of Loughborough and populated this with data from a number of sources including the UK government department DEFRA, The University of Cambridge and a series of commercially available databases. The figure that we used for paper/foil laminate packaging was 2.95 kg CO_2e/kg. A quick word on carbon figures. People tend to ask 'Is that figure good or bad?' and that's the wrong question. It is simply the figure. But what it allows us to do is compare against other options. I dig into the benefits and shortcomings of carbon as a totem for environmental impact later in this book, but at this point it is enough to say that while it is the best measure we have, and this figure is pretty useful, it reveals the shortcomings of all environmental metrics, as in this case the issue with carton-board is its recyclability. The packaging material is recyclable but usually the consumer would need to take these to a household waste recycling centre as they are mostly not included in kerbside recycling collections. Consequently this material is likely to end up in landfill and the value of its atoms will be lost.

GLASS

Glass is as old as the hills. It has many advantages and a couple of disadvantages. First up is protection. Glass contains and protects. It withstands gaseous pressure and therefore can be used for carbonated drinks. It is made from silica and usually has a lid of steel, aluminium, plastic or cork. Everyone loves glass as it is considered a natural material. But it has limitations. Firstly, it is really heavy. We will cover the implications of this shortly. Secondly, it breaks easily, so although it contains, it isn't the greatest in terms of protection.

Let's dig a little deeper. In terms of tessellation, bottles are circular so there is wasted space within secondary packaging; however, with no flat sides the pack is stronger. Moving onto embedded carbon impact, the impact per kg is pretty good at 1.54 kg CO_2e/kg (so this is lower than the figure for Tetra-type materials). But glass is heavy and this tends to make it less efficient than all of the other packaging materials we will look at in this section. Now, for recyclability, there are no problems here. Glass is one of the most recycled packaging materials with circa (estimates vary) 71 per cent of glass bottles being recycled in the UK.[2]

PET (POLYETHYLENE TEREPHTHALATE)

PET is the clear plastic that is used for packaging for water, sparkling drinks, juices and smoothies. It is incredibly light and protects the product well as it rarely breaks. It contains the product well and is more than capable of holding carbonated drinks. However, the material is slightly gas-permeable and leaks both oxygen and CO_2

over time. In terms of tessellation it is the same as glass with all PET bottles being cylindrical.

In terms of carbon impact it has a relatively low impact per kg and most packages require very small amounts of PET, hence it is often the best option from a carbon perspective.

All materials have an embedded carbon impact (the carbon locked up in the material and from its extraction) and there is also an impact dependent on the manufacturing process. So for PET the embedded carbon impact is 3.12 kg CO_2e/kg for moulded and 2.64 for extruded. This seems high, right? 3.12 kg is double the impact of glass. However, a plastic bottle is significantly lighter than a glass one, around 85 per cent lighter. Therefore the carbon impact per bottle is lower for PET than it is for glass. But what about recyclability? There is much nonsense spoken about plastic recycling, with the often quoted figure of 'only 8 per cent of all plastic made is recycled'. This is indeed rubbish (pun intended), so what are the facts? There are two plastic types that are widely recycled and one of those is PET. Currently around 75 per cent of all plastic bottles are recycled (although this incudes incineration with energy recovery).[3] The European average for recycling of PET bottles alone is 50 per cent. Not 8 per cent. That figure relates to all plastic produced, from carpets, to clothing, to building materials, to plastic in paint. Literally everything. This is one example of environmental alarmism and is not that helpful when it comes to making science-led decisions.

ALUMINIUM

Metal-based packaging is great from a containment and protection perspective. It works for carbonated drinks and the consumer likes it. Most beverage cans are now made of aluminium rather than steel. Again it has the same tessellation issues as all round containers. From a carbon perspective it is energy intensive at 11.9 kg CO_2e/kg for virgin aluminium. This falls considerably when recycled and it is thought that almost half of the aluminium in the general European supply is from recycled sources. This would give a carbon intensity figure of 6.64 kg CO_2e/kg. But let's stick with the virgin aluminium figure for this activity.

In terms of recyclability aluminium is recycled everywhere and the recycling rate across Europe is circa 72 per cent.[4]

So to summarize the impact in numbers:

TABLE 6.1   Beverage container materials comparison

Material	Carbon impact per kg	Recycling rate
Carton-board	2.95	25%
Glass	1.54	71%
PET	3.12	50%
Aluminium	11.9	72%

Looking at this you would be forgiven for thinking that we should put all drinks back in glass. But it isn't as simple as that. Let's insert some real packaging weights.

Looking at a comparison between these materials in real life we have a carton-board pack weighing 31 g, a glass bottle weighing 173 g, a PET bottle weighing 22 g and an aluminium can weighing 14 g. Let's see what that does to the comparison.

Now the table looks very different:

TABLE 6.2   Carbon impact of different beverage containers per container

Material	Carbon impact per kg	Recycling rate	Pack weight grams	Carbon impact per pack in grams
Carton-board	2.95	25%	31	91.45
Glass	1.54	71%	173	266.42
PET	3.12	50%	22	68.64
Aluminium	11.9	72%	14	166.6

Additionally, these packs have different volumes of liquid in them. Therefore, one further adjustment is required to divide the carbon impact by the volume of the drink to give a figure that represents packaging impact in carbon per unit of drink (ml in this case).

This exacerbates the difference:

TABLE 6.3 Carbon impact of different beverage containers per ml of product

Material	Carbon impact per kg	Recycling rate	Pack weight grammes	Carbon impact per pack in grammes	Volume of liquid (ml)	Carbon impact per ml
Carton-board	2.95	25%	31	91.45	500	0.18
Glass	1.54	71%	173	266.42	250	1.07
PET	3.12	50%	22	68.64	500	0.14
Aluminium	11.9	72%	14	166.6	330	0.50

If we are to measure environmental impact solely in carbon then the glass bottle has an impact over seven times greater than the plastic one. And that then leads us to the big question: Is carbon the best metric for understanding environmental impact?

Example 2: Trainers/sneakers

If I was to ask you who made the greenest sneakers/trainers what would you say? My guess is that you'd mention the one with the V on the side. Veja do a good job and they make a nice shoe. But of course the answer to this question is 'it depends how you measure it'. Veja make their shoes in Brazil and many use leather as the body of the shoe. This gives reasonable longevity and can be sourced from animals involved in regenerative agriculture. Then there are the ones made from wool: Allbirds. The interesting thing about this brand is the intellectual property they developed to make their midsole. They built a midsole using sugar cane and then offered to share the technology with other shoemakers. My guess is that you didn't think about Adidas or Nike. The reality is that every shoe brand has been working on this for decades and your choice depends upon the metric or issue that you're most concerned about.

Some manufacturers throw all their weight behind recycled materials. Adidas partnered with Parley to use oceanbound waste, Nike have their re-grind programme. For some it's a circular economy approach. Halo, Loop and On Running went this way.

But if we look at carbon – and given the climate emergency we are in it makes sense to do so – then you may be surprised.

The average shoe on the market has a carbon footprint of around 13.6 kg CO_2e per pair.[5] This figure is 10 years old now but still widely quoted. Allbirds quote an average figure of 12.5 kg.[6] A pair of leather Vejas weighs in at 21.5 kg CO_2e; Nike's best shoe is 90 per cent made from recycled materials, and comes in at 3.7 kg CO_2e, while Adidas (partnering with Allbirds) hit 2.94 kg CO_2e.

Once more we are left asking 'Is carbon the best way of determining environmental impact'? The answer is yes, it probably is. But it isn't the only way. You choose the thing you are most interested in and focus on that. But dive into the next section before you make your mind up.

One thing is for sure, the greenest shoe out there is the one you already own. Keep your stuff as long as you can, gift it when you're finished (if there is any life left in it), buy the lowest impact replacement aligned with your principles, don't confuse buying more stuff (even if it's green) with reducing your impact, and definitely don't use green consumption as a totem for being a good person or for virtue signalling.

How do we measure better?

I'm sure you've seen the image in Figure 6.1, or a similar one. Its purpose is to ask a bigger question regarding where we should focus our attention in the fight for a 'greener' world. And it raises some good questions. It attempts to identify some of the interconnections between these issues too.

The problem is that this type of image is used by some in the environmental movement to attack others in the same movement. I've been saying for some time now that

FIGURE 6.1   Carbon tunnel vision or carbon myopia schematic

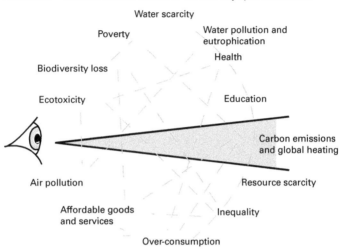

Source: Sourced from many such examples online

we can't afford friendly fire. We all want a better, safer and cleaner world that isn't warming; yet there is a real risk of in-fighting. Regenerative agriculture campaigners versus vegans; anti-plastic activists versus net-zero campaigners. This does nobody any good, and certainly not the planet. We need to avoid this at all costs.

Looking in more detail at Figure 6.1, it misses some important things out. I think it is worth looking at these as it helps us understand what 'better' or 'good' is and how easy it is to confuse or lead the consumer to think or believe what businesses want them to. The diagram talks of 'water scarcity' and that feels like drinking water. Indeed, we have a huge challenge ensuring that there is enough clean water for everyone. But it misses the ocean crisis: changes in the oceans and therefore their ability to regulate temperature, produce food and generate the oxygen that we breathe. The main threat to the oceans is heating and acidification, both solely driven by climate change and therefore carbon. Eutrophication (the gradual enrichment of a body of water, or portions of it, with minerals and nutrients, which results in dead water that will not support life as it once did) is directly linked to climate change and therefore carbon in two ways. Climate change and the temperature increase that seas are experiencing catalyses eutrophication by giving rise to conditions that increase nutrient loadings in aquatic habitats and support rapid algal growth. The complexity of natural feedback loops is on full display here. As eutrophication increases due to climate change it also reduces the ability and speed of water bodies to sequester carbon, thus exacerbating the problem. In a paper published in *ISME Communications* it is suggested that 'Climate change related prolonged warming will likely accelerate existing eutrophication effects'.[7] This link is not acknowledged in the diagram above.

Ecotoxicity is also directly linked to climate change and therefore carbon. In a recent paper Borgå et al. indicate that climate change impacts the long-range migration of air pollution resulting in, amongst other things, the concentration of pollution in sensitive Arctic wildlife.[8]

Affordable goods and services – this one is a bit vague to be honest. But if we narrow down on the hierarchy of needs and focus on shelter and food the cost of these and the availability are directly impacted by climate change and therefore carbon. The impact of climate change on harvest reliability and yield are noted elsewhere in this book. In terms of housing there is a direct link between the climate crisis and affordable housing.[9]

Overconsumption is obviously and clearly linked to carbon and climate change, not just in terms of the amount of 'stuff' we consume but also the type of stuff. As the world gentrifies, as populations become wealthier, the volume of things consumed increases and the impact of that stuff also increases. For example, we consume more meat and dairy per head and reduced calories from plants, own more electronic items and travel more and further.

Resource scarcity. It's no surprise to find that we tended to get the easiest to reach resources out of the ground first. The less available resources will have a greater environmental impact (in terms of carbon but also yield) than the more available. We are in a feedback loop with a lot of these issues but they are more interconnected than many argue.

Biodiversity loss is directly related to carbon. Climate change drives biodiversity loss and biodiversity loss reduces carbon sinks.

All of this impacts health in so many ways, from excess heat to the spread of malaria-carrying insects as the climate zones compress, the rise of other pandemics and disease, and the spread of tropical infectious diseases and vector-borne pathogens.

The reason that carbon as a metric has become dominant is because it is simpler to count than other sustainability measures. It is also a reasonable totem for other climate-heating gases. It is possible to calculate embedded carbon and hence include some sort of resource impact. Clearly transport is straightforwardly converted to carbon. The challenge comes in terms of waste. While we can use carbon to calculate waste treatment impact it is poor at taking into consideration accumulation in the environment and its subsequent impact.

FIGURE 6.2   Carbon 20:20 vision: How carbon and global heating impacts nearly everything

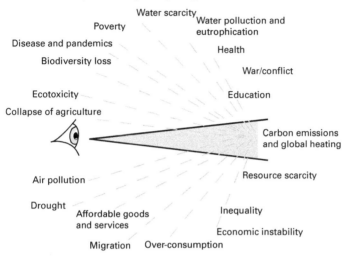

This is a really complex issue. When looking at plastic packaging, for example, this accumulates in the environment (particularly the oceans as that's where all rivers run) and has significant environmental impacts in terms of fish and sea life (although it is dwarfed in impact by climate change and over-fishing). If we were to move to glass the carbon impact and therefore global heating potential would rise five-fold. Which do we focus on? To me climate change is the largest and most urgent issue that we face. Furthermore, it connects to many other issues.

I've amended the 'carbon tunnel vision' diagram as shown in Figure 6.2. It's now more of a carbon 20:20 vision diagram. There are now many more connections and further categories of damage added.

CHAPTER SEVEN

The strategic tools you need to change your business

The next two chapters look at the tools you will need to change your business. This chapter deals with the more philosophical, strategic and policy tools and the following chapter deals with the practical and scientific tools. But, as all businesses should, we start with the consumer.

The rise of the environmentally conscious consumer has long been heralded but with scant evidence of it actually happening. Well, that's all changed.

There have been many surveys of consumers over the last decade that reveal an increase in awareness around sustainability and a shift in purchasing behaviours. In 2019 Edelman published its regular Trust Barometer and this found that one in two consumers define themselves as belief-driven consumers (they choose, switch, avoid or boycott a brand based on its stand on societal issues) with two-thirds of them buying a brand for the first time because of the brand's position on a controversial issue and the same proportion refusing to buy from a brand because it stayed silent on an issue it had an obligation to address.

Other research from Business Wire interviewed 10,000 people across 17 countries and found that 85 per cent of respondents have shifted their purchases towards more sustainable products and services.[1] This is particularly prevalent within Millennial and Gen-Z consumers, and as these groups continue to make up a larger share of the consumer demographic we should expect to see this trend strengthen.

PwC have also identified substance behind these trends.[2] Over half of the 9,180 consumers interviewed (from 25 countries) declare that they have become more eco-friendly. This is interesting but the most striking element is those countries that are leading the way. Shoppers in Indonesia (86 per cent), Vietnam and the Philippines (74 per cent each) and Egypt (68 per cent) top the 'I give a damn' chart. Deloitte and Forbes have also identified the same shifts in behaviour.

This is significant shift and is matched by the rise of the belief-driven employee, with 61 per cent of employees choosing their employer based on beliefs.[3] This concept of belief-driven behaviour is not new but it has caught the marketing world a little flat-footed.

I get asked by many of my clients: 'We've noticed a pref-erence for x in our market but it's not all men in their 20s or women in their 30s, or college educated. It seems random. Can you help us understand what's going on?' Yes of course I can. This is a challenge because business likes straight lines and clear Venn diagrams. As soon as we begin to talk about beliefs, we lose both of those.

But the reality in my experience is that we align with something, an approach, a philosophy, a vision, that a business projects more than the product. So if we are the kind of person that likes to back David over Goliath we will overlook the shortcomings of a (potentially) inferior product to back the approach we believe in. For example, we may not like the big soft drink manufacturers and therefore back the plucky start-up. We may use sugar as one of the buttress roots of this decision, even though there is more sugar in the Elderflower Presse that we're buying, or the heavy glass packaging is worse than the plastic bottle we are eschewing. These beliefs are really hard to determine. I've built a relatively simple model that allows brands to play with beliefs and how they align with aspiration and behaviour. This is described in Chapter 5. First I want to begin to reveal a set of sequential techniques that will allow you to change your business to do more good and less bad.

How to begin thinking about sustainability in your business

I'm going to take you through a series of practical steps that will help shape your thinking and your business (see Figure 7.1).

FIGURE 7.1 Steps in the development of a business environmental strategy

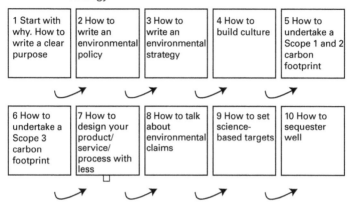

1 Start with why

People don't buy what you do, they buy why you do it. This is often cited because it's true. Simon Sinek brought it to our attention in his Ted Talk and book *Start with Why*. Sure, it's 13 years old now, sure you've heard it before but that doesn't make it less true. Describing why your business does what it does rather than leading with how it does what it does, or worse leading with what it does, creates a stickiness and personality for your brand. This makes you harder to forget but it also works to attract a customer who is interested in more than the cheapest product or service on offer.

Working out your why is akin to developing a philosophy that sits above the brand, or behind it. I define brand as the half-life of your business, how the business/product/service leaves you feeling afterwards. The why is the heartbeat of the business and brand. It is the reason you (as a business owner) do what you do, or why you (as an employee) work for the business you work for. It is the reason you get out of bed and get excited about work (tip: if you don't feel like this, it's best you change job sooner rather than later). I heartily recommend you watch the Ted Talk on this by Simon Sinek, but in essence the concept can be summarized thus: Having a clear why not only helps customers work out if they feel anything more than a transactional relationship with the brand, it also allows the brand to innovate freely and develop products and services aligned with their why rather than the thing they make. For example, Dell positioned itself as a computer manufacturer. As a result, when they tried to produce MP3 devices, they failed since no-one thought they could purchase an MP3 player from a computer business. But Apple, whose identity is defined by why they do what they do, was able to create an MP3 player as well as smart-phones and tablets. In short, stop selling the features that your product or service provide and start selling why you do what you do and how it makes people feel. Your objective is to attract customers who share your philosophy. You don't need to know how to stand out from the competitors. It is now a dialogue about various needs rather than an argument about better or worse.

What's this got to do with sustainability? Having a clear purpose changes your relationship with the customer, changes the way you talk about why, how and what you do and creates more space to talk about a perception beyond profit. Having a clear and sparkling purpose is a key element to developing products and services that have less impact and attracting customers who want to have less impact, or feel less bad about the impact of the things they buy.

The way you write a why is to get a bit hippy about things. I always start with two words: 'We believe...'. If you talk about the things you believe in its harder to slip into what you do or how you do it.

So start with 'We believe...' – Sinek himself says to start with 'Our why is to... so that...'. I don't have a problem with this but it is very easy to insert what it is that you do rather than why you do it.

Your Why Statement is the most efficient to articulate your purpose. It should be:

- simple and clear
- actionable
- focused on how you'll contribute to society
- expressed in positive language that resonates with you
- 'evergreen', meaning that it should be applicable to everything you do, both personally and professionally – without separation.

Try it. See what you get.

You may never say your why in public, in a presentation or write it on a website. But you might. And people should be able to feel it – it should run through the way you work.

2 How to write an environmental policy

Policy, policy, policy, boring, boring, boring.

Well, maybe. But if we write something down and publish it, then maybe we will do it. If it isn't written down, then it definitely won't be done.

An environmental policy outlines your commitment to reduce your impact on the environment, and provides a framework for setting objectives and targets to improve environmental performance.

There is no standard format for an environmental policy. The policy should be specific to your organization and relevant to its activities. It should be realistic, achievable and a serious commitment to reduce your environmental impact.

As a minimum your environmental policy should contain a commitment to:

- continually improve your environmental performance by monitoring progress against targets and objectives on a regular basis
- prevent pollution and reduce your impact on the environment
- comply with relevant environmental legislation

Due to the climate emergency there is now the potential legal requirement (in numerous countries and states) to set carbon reduction or net-zero pathways. Therefore it is recommended that your policy acknowledge this in some way. The most basic assessment you can do here is a Scope 1 and 2 assessment of your company's carbon impact. This will be discussed in greater detail later but in essence Scope 1 covers direct emissions from owned or controlled sources (gas, vehicle fuels, etc.). Scope 2 covers indirect emissions from the generation of purchased electricity, steam, heating and cooling consumed by the reporting company. This is a pretty straightforward set of calculations to undertake and I will cover them in detail later. If you aren't currently legislated to report your Scope 1 and 2 emissions it is likely that in the next five years you will be.

But you need to think more widely.

You may also want to include commitments relating to:

- efficient use of water and energy
- efficient use of other natural resources
- recycling
- minimizing waste
- sustainable transport
- responsible purchasing
- minimizing noise disturbance
- use of non-toxic products
- working with clients and suppliers to encourage high environmental standards
- raising awareness and training employees on environmental issues

You set your aspirations in a policy and outline how you will meet them: what procedures do you have in place to achieve them?

Depending upon your sector I would also consider net gain. Biodiversity net gain is an approach to development (but also business) that leaves biodiversity in a better state than before. So if you are in the construction sector this clearly applies to you. But if you are in the agricultural, food, natural textiles or timber sector, and many more, it also applies to you.

Start your environmental policy with a brief outline of your organization and its activities. A little introduction to your company and why you set it up, and perhaps introduce your why at this point, but gently.

Follow this with a general statement of your environmental aims and a list of your environmental objectives, including brief details of how these will be achieved.

This is a formal document but don't forget to give it some of your personality. The way I do this is by writing a policy statement, something like Method's 'We fight dirty. We believe in proudly doing business with a purpose, and that good design has the power to change the world.' I would then move into the detail.

Things to consider in your policy: A checklist

The checklist below may help you to draft a policy appropriate to your business. Choose examples of the statements that would apply to your business and make the statements as specific as possible for your operations:

- Comply with environmental legislation and other requirements. This may seem obvious but many businesses don't. The waste regulations are particularly easy to miss as are packaging and other producer responsibility obligations as they tend to be based on the size of your business and therefore kick in as you grow.
- Recognize the importance of environmental issues to your business. A little philosophical but your supply chain is subject to environmental risks. It is worth recognizing this.

- Assess the environmental impact of all historic, current and likely future operations. We have moved to carbon as a totem for wider environmental impact and you should definitely include any Scope 1 and 2 assessment. But also widen this to identify your land, air, water and biodiversity impacts.

- Continually seek to improve environmental performance, with regular checks on progress. Setting targets here is difficult. You can make the statement that you will continually improve but it is important to say how you will measure this. Using carbon is straightforward and I would calculate the carbon impact per unit of turnover or per square meter of space. This allows you to de-couple growth and impact.

- Aim to reduce pollution, emissions and waste. Again the key here is measuring these.

- Reduce the use of all raw materials, energy and supplies. Once more this needs to be proportioned to turnover or premises size.

- Raise awareness, encourage participation and train employees in environmental matters. Introducing basic carbon literacy training is a good place to start.

- Demand similar environmental standards from all suppliers and contractors. Having effective supply chain environmental management is a standard part of the contract.

- Assist customers to use your products and services in an environmentally sensitive way. Often (especially in the case of energy-using products) the use-phase of the product has a significant impact. Hence some guidance on how to use the product more efficiently is sensible.

- Liaise with the local community, particularly if you're manufacturing on-site or have other environmental impacts including transport, noise or light, or if you are planning to expand.
- Participate in discussions about environmental issues internally. Build sustainability into both board, operations and financial meetings.
- Communicate environmental aims and objectives to employees and external stakeholders. Don't just have a notice board, actually engage the team. They will have the best ideas on how to reduce impact.
- Agree to commit to environmental principles and continual improvement.

You must also then keep your environmental policy up to date. To check that your company's current activities still comply with your environmental policy, it's a good idea to carry out a regular review – usually on an annual basis. These are key to ensuring that there is continual improvement in environmental performance.

Bear in mind that if your business activities or operations change significantly, the policy may need to be amended.

The challenge with all policy documents is that they get written and forgotten. The way I'd go about this is to talk to the team about the things they think are important and should be in the policy. Then look at the best policies of others. Don't stick to your own sector, think tangentially. Then repeat the staff engagement piece annually. The environmental policy should be available for all employees to read.

Extending the scope of your policy

Your environmental policy doesn't have to exist in isolation. In fact, it can be useful to extend the scope of your policy to cover corporate social responsibility and sustainable development. You could choose to develop this either within a single policy or create separate, linked policies. An extended policy acknowledges the fact that different groups of people rely on your business and outlines how you go about minimizing your impact on the environment.

By developing a corporate social responsibility policy, you are showing that you are:

- Dealing with suppliers and employees in a responsible way – for example by being open and honest about your products and services and avoiding pressure selling. It also means going beyond the legal minimum when dealing with employees and promoting best practice.
- Building up a good relationship with the local community – for example by supporting a local charity or sponsoring a local event.
- Minimizing your impact on the environment and cutting pollution and waste – by using energy efficiency measures, e.g. switching off lights, reducing the use of water. You could also consider minimizing waste and reducing the environmental impact of your business generally, e.g. buying locally to cut fuel costs.

Equally, you can show that you take sustainable development seriously by:

- Considering the life cycle of your products and services and designing them to be as sustainable as possible.

- Buying materials and resources that come from renewable sources.
- Reusing or recycling your waste or passing it on to other businesses to use as a resource.
- Going beyond your legal obligations and anticipating changes so that you can make adjustments before legislation comes into force.
- Involving employees and other stakeholders in sustainable development – by involving them in training and incentives to encourage buy-in to your strategy.

In recent years the three letters ESG (environment, social, governance) have emerged as one of the new approaches to embedding sustainability into the corporate world. It's pretty easy to be cynical about this stuff and dismiss it as corporate gobbledegook and just lip-service to sustainability. In reality they are a great way of managing risk and this was a big part of the development of this approach. Sustainability is seen, as previously mentioned, as a risk to brand and PR. It is also a risk to investment, financial security, supply chain security and business continuity. My view is that we are in such a precarious and urgent position that it doesn't really matter what motivations business have, as long as they do something. We need to stop fighting amongst ourselves at this stage and celebrate all positive action.

Breaking the individual elements of ESG down in greater detail, the environmental element covers how a business performs in terms of management, protection and enhancement of:

- waste and pollution
- resource depletion

- greenhouse gas emissions
- deforestation
- climate change
- raw material use

The social element looks at how the company treats people within and outside of the business. It includes:

- employee relations and diversity
- working conditions, including child labour and slavery within the supply chain
- local community impact, both minimizing impact and enhancing the local community and communities local to the supply chain
- health and safety
- industrial relations

The third element is governance criteria, which considers how a corporation regulates and polices itself and how the company is governed. This focuses on:

- tax strategy
- executive remuneration
- diversity of the board
- political lobbying
- corruption and bribery
- donations
- ethics

Increasingly ESG policies and strategies are seen as a go/ no-go decision gate for external investment. Consequently sustainability will become crucial to business management and business growth whether or not the business is committed to improved environmental performance.

So you've got a policy – you can use it in tenders and contracts, you can pop it in a frame and hang it in the visitor's area, but my main advice is to make it work and change the behaviour, practices and culture of the business. To do this you need a strategy.

3 How to write an environmental strategy

A strategy is a set of time-bound initiatives that take a company from where they are to where they want to be. Therefore, the first step is to define where you want to be. What is your vision? It is useful to refer back to your 'why' at this stage. What kind of business does the world need right now? How can you be a part of that and still make a profit? I've included a series of steps and templates to help with this.

Step 1: How to write a sustainability vision.

This is the first step. What do you stand for? You may already have a very clear idea and if so that's fine. But if not, you could work through the following template.

VALUES
The first step is to work out what it is you stand for. We covered this earlier so you may have written this down; if so go and find it. If not it is time to do it now. It can help to start with the things you stand against. Then the things

you stand for. This could be a simple statement like 'Having a net-zero impact' or 'Becoming a regenerative business'. Or it could be more specific like 'Ensuring a living wage throughout the supply chain'. Remember you are going to need to put things in place to make this happen.

CHANGE

What kind of change do you want to be part of? You can reflect statements of other companies here. You can align yourself with the mission of others here – Seedlip on no alcohol drinking or Microsoft on regenerative agriculture, for example.

ACTION

What are you going to do about this? I'm looking for broad-brush things here rather than specific practical tasks, that's for later. Think 'We will be net zero by 2030', or 'We will phase out all use of solvents by 2028'. That kind of thing.

SUMMING IT UP

The aim of this is to condense everything into a one- or two-line statement.

This kind of thing: 'We believe that there is no business without nature. Our vision is to go beyond compliance and become a net-zero business by 2030 and a regenerative business by 2040.'

I've included a simple canvas that may help order your thoughts (see Figure 7.2).

FIGURE 7.2 Sample canvas

Your sustainability vision

Your values		What kind of change do we want to be part of?
We stand against	We stand for	
To create a more sustainable world we will...		Sum it up in one sentence

Step 2: Your environmental impacts

Next you need to summarize your environmental impacts. We will do this in detail later so this is just a summary. These will (at this stage) be simply a list. Such as:

- carbon emissions from energy consumption
- embedded carbon in raw materials and products
- transport impacts
- waste produced on-site
- product waste
- packaging impact

You will have a reasonable idea of where your impacts are. Trust your gut. When we build the carbon assessment later we will quantify and prioritize these, but at this stage just get them down. Our strategy will address them all and while we will look at the issues that are dominant in your business it is almost certain that the priority will be carbon, given the pressing urgency of the climate emergency and the knock-on impacts in terms of biodiversity and food production.

Step 3: What do your customers care about?

Then we move onto the concerns of your customers. Whether you trade business-to-business (B2B) or business-to-consumer (B2C) you need an understanding of the concerns of your end user. There is a real risk here for B2B businesses who are reliant on their business customer for visibility to the end user. I've seen this cause significant issues if your business customer isn't asking the right question of the end user. I've got around this in two different ways. First, I have worked with the business that sits between my client and the customer to better understand the customer interests. Second, I have undertaken primary research into the target market to understand consumer desires, fears and perceptions. What we find is that the end consumer reflects and amplifies the issues that make the headlines in the media, and particularly plastic. Therefore, there may be a need for customer education.

In order to widen the discussion it can be useful to give them a list of issues to rank. Something like that is shown in Table 7.1.

Then ask which is most important to them and which do they think you should address in your strategy. I find it useful to multiply these two scores by each other to get a prioritized score.

Step 4: Policy refinement

Now I want you to go back to your environmental policy. My guess is that it is still a little long and would benefit

TABLE 7.1 Customer environmental issues scoring

Environmental issue	Is it important to you (1–10, 1 being no and 10 being really important to you)	Do you think we have an obligation to address it? (1–10, 1 being 'not really' and 10 being 'hell yes')	Total. Multiply the scores by each other
Climate change			
Biodiversity loss			
Waste			
Plastic			
Soil collapse			
Air pollution			
Water pollution			
Population			
Resource use			
Compliance			

from some editing. This is the time. Words are beautiful, more words are not more beautiful: take as many out as possible. Simplify this as much as you are able. And write it on the canvas.

Step 5: Ideas

This is an out-and-out creativity session. For this you will need to talk to the rest of your team or your colleagues. There are three ways of having better ideas. I use these methods in my sustainability, innovation and strategy workshops. I'll explain them then I will add a fourth way.

ASK A BETTER QUESTION.

Better answers come from better questions. This is true, but what does it mean and how do you ask better questions?

I call my method the Stop, Look and Listen approach.

First off you **Stop**. You stop trying to solve what you think is the problem and sit and look at it from all angles. Pull together a group of people with a broad background. Introduce a very general challenge and get the group to write down and share what they feel about the challenge (or opportunity) without solving it. Then, in order, get them to ask questions about the challenge/opportunity. Give them a set amount of time to do this collectively – maybe 5–10 minutes. There are three rules. No-one is allowed to ask why anyone else is asking the question. No-one is allowed to say 'yes, but…', and no-one is allowed to proffer an answer. At the end of the session see how everyone feels about the challenge and see which of the questions need more analysis. This helps define or reframe the problem.

Then **Look**.

Get out: get out of your office/studio; get out of your building; get out of your sector. What is going on out there that you can learn from and how does what you see reframe your questions? I talked of this earlier but it bears repeating. Get out, look at what the world is doing, take questions back with you. Staying inside your business and trying to innovate there is like sitting in the car with the air circulation switched on, you will start to breathe your own exhaled breath and your windows will steam up. You need to see where you are going. Get out and look – at least wind the window down.

Next – **Listen.** Listen to your team, especially those who are closest to the customer; listen to your gut about the direction that the market is heading; more importantly listen to tangential markets. Where are they? What can you learn? What has got in their way? What trends do you see there? Keep your radar on always.

TALK TO PEOPLE NOT LIKE YOU
Similar people give similar answers to the same question. Talk to people not like you. Clearly talking to your customer helps but also talk to people from groups that you'd like to be your customer. Internally promote a diverse set of talents among employees. In your customer research try not to use customer recruitment agencies – they tend to deliver the same type of person. Find people yourselves.

MEDITATE
When we are in the meditation brainwave pattern (theta brainwaves) we are at our most creative. These come when we are 'not thinking', in a relaxed state. That's why many people have their best ideas just before sleep or in the

shower, on a walk or while gardening, swimming or during meditation. We can encourage these brainwaves by a little breath work or meditation. I build a little qigong into my workshops. This is a set of flowing meditative moves and breathing. It nudges the brain into theta. It works.

I said I would add a fourth approach. I call this 'three great and three crap ideas'. I encourage crap ideas, why? Well, when we remove the pressure of having killer ideas and encourage our brains to take a flight of fancy into the preposterous we free our imagination. I do this exercise with my biggest clients and while there is sometimes scepticism, we uncover gold in the crap ideas. Try it. It has never failed me.

These ideas could be thematic: 'develop a modular design for the homes we build in order to reduce waste and decrease construction time' or 'put all products in shippable boxes to remove one layer of packaging'. This is a quick-fire list that will change regularly as your strategy emerges and develops However, I recommend digging a little deeper here and outlining the rough timescales to deliver these ideas and maybe even include a name of someone who will have responsibility for this.

I've included a template, a canvas for the strategy that allows it to be displayed and understood quickly (see Figure 7.3). I'm not a fan of massive tomes that won't get read. I would rather have a single sheet that everyone understands and has access to. I would even use this in tender documents or as part of a proposal. However, if you prefer a more formal approach feel free to turn this into a written document in the traditional sense.

FIGURE 7.3   Environmental strategy canvas

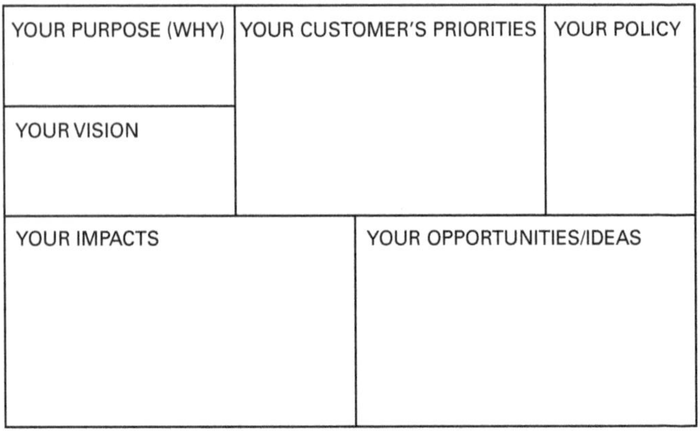

YOUR PURPOSE (WHY)	YOUR CUSTOMER'S PRIORITIES	YOUR POLICY
YOUR VISION		
YOUR IMPACTS	YOUR OPPORTUNITIES/IDEAS	

It is really important that this remains a living document that is not just written and filed away but becomes part of the culture. Let's look at culture now.

4   Building a culture that embeds sustainability into the business

What is culture? What is business culture?

Culture is the ideas, customs, practices and social behaviour of a group of people. So business culture is the ideas, customs, practices and behaviours of a business. We see examples of good business culture where ideas are valued and voices listened to, and we see examples of poor business cultures where enthusiasm and ideas are swatted like flies. I've worked in both cultures and something in-between. It all starts with the leadership. It doesn't always end there, however. I've seen culture dictated and built from other parts of an organization, although in my experience that has only happened when the leaders left a culture vacuum. Nature abhors a vacuum and something has to fill it. The worst culture I worked in was in a large supermarket. I'm sure they'd say that I didn't fit the 'big business' culture, but in reality I didn't thrive in a culture that verged on bullying and posturing; one where trust and accountability were in short measure. The reality was that I only saw my kids awake on the weekends. No-one does well in those situations. I've also been lucky to work in great cultures, where ideas were valued and nurtured, people supported, and in whose culture ideas and skills grew. What was the difference between those organizations? In one I had a boss who didn't trust anyone, micro-managed everyone, and who was fundamentally unhappy with who she was. In the other organization my boss was trusting, knew that we would do our best work when we felt confident rather than bullied, and didn't let his ego get in the way of the team. Both teams produced notable and good work, but they did so in different ways. The main difference is that everyone wanted to give their best for the second organization and everyone was scared of losing their job in the first organization. Fear or trust? Which is the best motivator? Which is the healthiest? Which helps attract and retain the best talent in the world?

So how do you build a 'good' culture?

It starts with a clear and well-communicated vision. Sustainability has been erroneously, or mischievously, placed in opposition to business interests for decades. As discussed earlier in this book, this is folly and increasingly no longer the case. But building the business case, understanding the brand and marketing benefits, and being able to articulate the talent attraction and retention benefits to the business is really important, so make this high-definition business case and make it visible.

The culture of an organization revolves around its employees. Therefore, it is vital that they understand what sustainability is and how it affects their roles and work. It's also really important to communicate that this is a marathon rather than a sprint. Long gone are the days when a business could attain ISO9001 (a quality systems standard) or ISO14001 (an environmental systems standard) in under two weeks by paying someone to do it. Showing how employee habits and behaviours impact sustainability in day-to-day work helps the team begin to understand the complexity of sustainability.

When your people rock up at work they don't leave their ethics and morals in a bag by the door to collect as they leave. All employees can add great insight and dynamism to a sustainability effort and the culture of the business. Everyone pulling in the same direction results in a significant force. Being able to unify a personal ethics and business ethics creates a unity of purpose that encourages people to stay with a business longer.

Here's a story, a true one. I was working with a company. A high street name. I was running a workshop on purpose and brand rather than sustainability. However, sustainability came up as something on which the business needed more action and a stronger position. I mooted this. Most of the team agreed apart from one person, a senior person. They said that their data indicated that their customers weren't engaged in sustainability, that it wasn't a driver for them to visit the stores. Oh, I thought, that's a bit short-sighted. I was just about to explain why I thought so when a young intern at the back of the room piped up: 'If you don't do something on sustainability I won't ever work for you,' she said. Mic drop. The senior leader changed their mind. Embedding sustainability into your business, into your culture, doesn't just make you more competitive and lift your brand; it isn't just the right thing to do morally; if you don't do it then your employees won't work for you. This also illustrates the value of insight over data.

The company can further advance its sustainability culture by making sure their key performance indicators (KPIs) and rewarding systems also include sustainability criteria. When Marks & Spencer introduced their Plan A programme they insisted that every product sold had to have one Plan A attribute. This embedded sustainability into every buyer's job description. So they didn't have a small team looking after sustainability, they had the whole company. Furthermore, it is important to incentivize performance in sustainability. This sends a clear message to employees that sustainability is a priority and sustainable progress is valued as part of the organization's culture. This is how you create a series of sustainability leaders throughout the business.

Measure to manage

After you've begun to make the business case in the widest possible sense, it's time to start measuring your impact and begin to understand what this means. We have a detailed section coming up on carbon footprinting your Scope 1, 2 and 3 impacts. Start with Scope 1 and 2.

You only manage what you measure, so having a clear understanding of your impacts is non-negotiable. Additionally (depending on your size) you may have a legal requirement to report this data. Measurement also allows you to set targets – targets won't get hit if they are never set. Having clear, well-communicated and maybe even public targets tends to focus the mind.

The key to building a culture is to create a compelling vision and build trust. But there is also something about the way a space is designed and used. Clearly small cubicles and hushed tones are really unpleasant to experience, but likewise beanbags and open spaces don't work for everyone either. The nirvana in terms of design is to have clear zones. A deep work zone where people can go to sink into work without the distractions of a shared space. Then there needs to be a more communal space with great light and a larger shared table where conversation is encouraged. And, of course, the all-important kitchen where we often find more time to chat with others and particularly others not in your team/immediate vicinity. The smoking room/space used to provide this. I genuinely know people who started smoking just to be able to get the fast-track on promotions, news and gossip. Just think about that. What kind of closed and segmented culture gives rise to a series of behaviours that push people into a health-damaging habit to feel connected to the team/leadership?

Now you need to take this stuff to the board. They need to not only approve it but to see the deep commercial value here. This may be a harder job than any other in this process.

It is important to develop ideas and actions that the team can implement. Some of these will be micro (recycling policies, purchasing policies, etc.) and some macro (investment in new capital equipment or buildings). All are welcome. Meet regularly in teams to harvest and stimulate as many ideas as possible. When you implement these ideas track the benefits financially and environmentally. Celebrate even the smallest win, especially if the idea came from the wider team. The team sit closer to the daily problems and challenges, and are usually best-placed to solve them.

Here's another story. I once worked with a large engineering and manufacturing company. They made hundreds of different products and the team were incredibly talented. The management got me in to look at how to reduce costs by implementing a blend of green and lean (lean manufacturing is closely related to waste minimization, which was one of the first attempts to embed sustainability into business; it espouses a lean production process that removes physical waste and lost time in order to increase yield). I looked around and drew a process flow diagram (more on that shortly) then came up with 10 or so ideas. They were pleased. I asked them how often they engaged the team and asked for ideas, given the fact that the team have to deal with the same problems every single day. 'Well, we tried that. We put a suggestion box on the wall but no-one used it.' Hmm I thought, that's odd. So I checked. The team had been amazing all morning with me. I know a little bit about a lot of things having worked with over 1,000 businesses in my career, so I can speak the manufacturing and process language fluently. I'm also really curious and ask loads of questions, in a nice way. Therefore people often give their best and the team had been amazing. So I asked 'How do you suggest new ideas and improvements?'

'Oh,' they said, 'well there was a suggestion box but we put loads of ideas in and they're still in there. No-one opened it.' And true enough, I got the box opened and it was full of ideas. The leadership had checked it at the end of the first week and it was indeed empty. They never checked it again. This is so short-sighted. The apocryphal story of the 3M employee developing Post-it Notes as a result of a faulty batch of court tape indicates how a culture of suggestion and innovation can build great ideas. If you're going to ask the team for input, please look at it, respond and celebrate.

So here's a checklist to help build a sustainability culture:

1 Develop a clear vision around sustainability. How does it support and enhance your business strategy?
2 Communicate this to the team and ask for their input.
3 Build sustainability into the fabric of KPIs and rewards.
4 Get a measure of your impact and communicate this to the team.
5 Develop realistic and science-based targets.
6 Match your workspace to your vision of the culture.
7 Communicate this to the board and gain their support and vision.
8 Run a series of ideas sessions with the team to engage but also flush out ideas.
9 Celebrate each win.

CHAPTER EIGHT

The practical and science-based tools to change your business (and still make a profit)

Having a great idea, a clear strategy, an aspiration isn't enough anymore. Writing it on a wall or the side of your building isn't enough anymore. You need to do something. I'd say at this stage, you need to do anything.

The place to start is to understand what your environmental impacts are. The way we do this is to undertake an environmental audit or a carbon footprint. The latter is mandatory in many countries for businesses over a certain size and consequently this is where we will focus.

I've already talked about whether carbon is the best metric and my view is that it is the best we have, the closest to a universal measure. This doesn't mean it is perfect. Far from it. But it is the way most of the world quantifies impact and I will now go through how to do that.

How to undertake a Scope 1 and 2 carbon footprint

All the way through this book I've talked about measurement. In order to bring sustainability to the boardroom there has to be measurable impact. This is perhaps frustrating as it tends to result in everything being boiled down to a carbon figure. As discussed earlier this can raise hackles with many people as they see it as too narrow, and I get that. However, as demonstrated earlier there is a demonstrative link between carbon and most other sustainability issues.

I think it worthwhile here to consider the role of experts in all of this. The last five years has seen a move away from science as a source of independent expertise and we've even seen a move away from experts in general. In the run-up to the calamitous Brexit vote in the UK in 2016 Britain reached fever pitch with a general fatigue and distrust of experts. This parallels the rise of the post-truth politician and the post-truth expert. In this period we have seen the rise of 'alternative facts', many surrounding climate change. These are easily debunked. However, we have also seen the rise of the non-expert influencer. Generally they speak about the urgent need to address environmental collapse but lack any detailed or scientific knowledge, hence they tend to echo media views on the main environmental issues which, in turn, are portrayed in such a way to sell media. I know bloggers, podcasters and TV 'experts' who have no background in sustainability or science. This is dangerous as it risks undermining the very cause they are trying to promote. There is a real need for clearly explained science and if these opinion-formers can come together with the scientific community maybe we can begin to make some progress.

All things considered, carbon is the best metric we currently have for environmental impact and that's why the vast majority of environmental assessment tools use it as a totem. This will change with the advent of net gain as a concept, however. Watch this space.

How do you undertake a carbon impact assessment?

Firstly what is a carbon impact assessment (also known as a carbon footprint)? A carbon assessment calculates the overall greenhouse gas (GHG) emissions that a person, group, occasion, business, organization or thing causes, both directly and indirectly. Through undertaking a carbon assessment you will gain a better understanding of your main sources of emissions as well as your options for reducing them. It presents a great starting point to compare your progress against and gives you the chance to create a plan for reducing your impact. Understanding where you are carbon inefficient can help identify areas where you are also financially inefficient.

In terms of methodology there are a number of stand-ards in different countries that can be applied to the process.

However, the overriding guidance here is known as the Greenhouse Gas (GHG) Protocol. The protocol is a partnership between the World Business Council for Sustainable Development and the World Resources Institute. It has established approaches and frameworks for the measurement of GHG emissions. We apply the GHG Protocol to all carbon assessments we deliver.

Before we delve into the details of carbon accounting, it is essential that we first establish organizational and operational boundaries. The former of these are typically high-level boundaries that regulate which business operations fall into the GHG inventory. In essence, which operations or facilities a company includes within their environmental impact assessment. There are various approaches here, such as equity share, operational control or financial control. For example, within an operational control approach, a company accounts for the carbon equivalent emissions associated with all operations for which it has operational control; however, operational control does not necessarily require sole authority or capacity for decision making.

Once the organizational boundary has been determined, we need to then look at defining the operational boundaries. Operational boundaries are determined by the 'scopes' of GHG emissions. There are three scopes, Scope 1, 2 and 3. Each scope categorizes direct or indirect emissions associated with the operations of a business. Definitions of each scope are as follows:

- Scope 1: Direct emissions which occur from sources which are owned or controlled by the reporting company.

- Scope 2: Indirect emissions which are associated with the generation of purchased energy by the reporting company.
- Scope 3: Indirect emissions which are as a result of the operations of the reporting company but are not owned or controlled by the reporting company; hence, not included within Scope 2.

Scope 1

Scope 1 GHG emissions are emissions associated with the following categories:

- Stationary combustion
- Fugitive emissions
- Mobile combustion

Stationary combustion refers to the emission of GHGs from stationary fuel combustion, typically that of solid fuel, liquid or gaseous fuel. This combustion is generally associated with the generation of electricity or heat. To quantify the GHG emissions associated with combustion of fuels, you would need to multiply the consumption of fuels by the relevant GHG conversion factor. An example of this might be 100 kWh (Gross CV) of natural gas, with a corresponding conversion factor of 0.18397 kg CO_2e/kWh (according to the 2022 DEFRA conversion factors), resulting in the emission of 18.397 kg CO_2e.

Fugitive emissions relate to GHG emissions resulting from the leakage or service of refrigeration and air conditioning units over their operational life and disposal. To calculate the GHG emissions associated with the service of refrigeration and air conditioning units, you would need to multiply the mass of refrigerant purchased, or consumed within servicing, by the relevant conversion factor. An example of this might be the re-gassing of 1 kg of R410A refrigerant, with a corresponding conversion factor of 2088 kg CO_2e/kg according to the 2022 DEFRA conversion factors, resulting in the emission of 2.088 tCO_2e.

In addition to this, to calculate the rate of fugitive emission leakage from the operational life of refrigeration and air conditioning units, you need to multiply the number of specific units by their equipment charge capacity, by the time used during the reporting period (years), by the annual leak rate (%), and then by the relevant GHG conversion factor. This will result in total kg CO_2e emissions associated with the service losses and equipment leaks over the full life of the equipment. To summarize, the calculation is:

No. units × Equipment charge capacity (kg) × Time used during the reporting year (years) × Annual leak rate (%) × Global warming conversion factor (kg CO_2e/kg) = Total kg CO_2e

An example of this might be the use of a domestic refrigeration unit, with a charge capacity of 1 kg of R410A. This refrigeration unit might have been used for six months out of the reporting year, with an estimated annual leak rate of 0.3 per cent according to Gov.uk environmental reporting guidelines. Plugged into the formula, this is displayed as:

$1 \times 1 \times 0.5 \times 0.3\% \times 2088$ kg CO_2e/kg = 3.132 kg CO_2e

Mobile combustion emissions relate to the direct emissions which are associated with the use of owned or leased mobile sources that are within a company's inventory boundary. To calculate the GHG emissions associated with this mobile combustion, you might collect data regarding the quantity of fuel consumed within the reporting year by these mobile sources. You would then multiply the quantity of this fuel consumed by the relevant GHG conversion factors. An example of this might be the consumption of 100 litres of petrol (average biofuel blend) over the reporting period, multiplied by the relevant GHG conversion factor of 2.16 kg CO_2e/L according to the 2022 DEFRA conversion factors, resulting in the emission of 216.185 kg CO_2e.

An alternative method would be to collect data regarding the distance travelled by each mobile source within the reporting year, as well as the vehicle specifications of these sources. An example of this might be 100 miles driven by a 'small car' fuelled by petroleum, multiplied by the relevant GHG conversion factor of 0.2358 kg CO_2e/mile, resulting in associated emissions of 23.58 kg CO_2e.

Scope 2

Scope 2 GHG emissions are associated with only one emissions category. This is emissions from purchased energy.

These emissions are indirect, as they are a consequence of the operations of the reporting company, yet they occur at sources owned or controlled by an outside entity. When calculating the environmental impact associated with this section, it is important that companies report on both their market-based and location-based emissions.

Market-based emissions encompass specific choices relating to energy suppliers, or the contract between supplier and consumer. The emissions factors used within this are supplier-specific and often reflect the emissions profiles associated with that of renewable electricity. Location-based emissions are calculated through the utilization of average GHG conversion factors from the electricity grids which supply the reporting facility.

Reporting companies should calculate and report on both their market and location-based emissions totals. A reporting company should select either market or location-based emissions as a baseline for tracking emissions over time, measuring year-on-year performance or setting emissions targets. If using market-based emissions as a measure of performance or setting of targets, this electricity should be verified through a scheme such as the Renewable Energy Guarantee of Origin certificate.

An example of market-based emissions might be a reporting company which consumes 1,000 kWh of electricity from a renewable electricity tariff with a fuel mix consisting of entirely offshore wind generated electricity. When multiplied by a relevant GHG conversion factor of 0.012 kg CO_2e/kWh electricity according to the life cycle emissions associated with offshore wind power published by the IPCC, this results in associated market-based emissions of 12 kg CO_2e.

An example of location-based emissions might be the same reporting company which consumes 1,000 kWh of electricity from the same renewable electricity tariff, multiplied by the average emissions intensity of the UK national grid, of which the relevant conversion factor is 0.19338 kg CO_2e/kWh according to the 2022 DEFRA conversion factors, resulting in associated location-based emissions of 193.38 kg CO_2e.

How to undertake a Scope 3 carbon footprint

Scope 3 GHG emissions encompass those that are associated with the reporting company's operations yet are not owned or controlled by the reporting company. Scope 3 emissions are all indirect emissions (excluding those reported in Scope 2) that occur in the reporting company's value chain. The GHG Protocol describes 15 GHG emissions categories within the Scope 3 boundary. These are:

1   purchased goods and services
2   capital goods
3   fuel and energy related activities not included in Scope 1 or Scope 2
4   upstream transport and distribution
5   waste generated in operations
6   business travel
7   employee commuting
8   upstream leased assets
9   downstream transport and distribution
10 processing of sold products
11 use of sold products
12 end-of-life treatment of sold products
13 downstream leased assets
14 franchises
15 investments

Prior to the assessment and calculation of GHG emissions associated with each of these categories, companies must identify the categories that are most relevant to their operations. The GHG Protocol criteria for identifying relevant Scope 3 categories are size, influence, risk, stakeholders, outsourcing, sector guidance, spending or revenue analysis, as well as other additional criteria. For greater depth into the description of activities relating to these criteria, see the GHG Protocol Technical guidance for calculating Scope 3 emissions.

It would require too much space and time here to give a comprehensive description of the contents, relevance and carbon accounting methodologies underlying the Scope 3 emissions categories. Therefore, I have summarized each of the 15 Scope 3 emissions categories listed in the GHG Protocol.

Purchased goods and services

This emissions category captures the GHG emissions associated with the goods and services purchased or acquired by the reporting company during the reporting year. These emissions relate to the extraction, processing, production, as well as transportation of goods and services. The calculation of these GHG emissions might be through quantification of cradle-to-gate GHG inventory data provided by the supplier of these goods or services, or through a spend-based method whereby the reporting company would estimate GHG emissions associated with the purchase of goods and services based on their economic value and relevant secondary emissions factors. These secondary emissions factors could take the form of GHG emissions per monetary value of the goods or services.

Capital goods

This emissions category captures the GHG emissions associated with the purchase or acquisition of capital goods by the reporting company during the reporting year. Similar to the first emissions category, these emissions relate to the extraction, production and transportation of capital goods. Again, the calculation of these GHG emissions might be through cradle-to-gate GHG inventory data, or a spend-based method.

Fuel and energy related activities (not included in Scope 1 or Scope 2)

This emissions category captures the GHG emissions associated with energy or fuels which are purchased or acquired by the reporting company during the reporting year, which aren't captured within the Scope 2 emissions category. This category would typically account for the upstream emission of purchased fuels and electricity, as well as the transmissions and distribution losses relating to the generation of purchased electricity, steam, heating or cooling. This category would also encompass the emissions associated with the generation of purchased electricity which is sold to end users; however, this would only be applicable to utility companies and energy retailers.

Upstream transport and distribution

This emissions category captures the GHG emissions associated with the transport and distribution of products which have been purchased during the reporting year. This transport and distribution might be between the reporting company's own operations and that of their tier 1 suppliers in vehicles not owned or controlled by the reporting company. Otherwise, it might be transport and distribution services by a third party which were purchased by the reporting company during the reporting year, including both inbound and outbound logistics, as well as transport and distribution between facilities owned or controlled by the reporting company.

Waste generated in operations

This emissions category captures the GHG emissions associated with the third-party disposal and treatment of the waste generated by the business operations of the reporting company during the reporting year. Not only does this emissions category capture GHG emissions associated with the disposal of solid waste, but it also captures those associated with wastewater.

While types of waste and methods of waste management are likely to differ depending on the operations of the reporting company, it is likely that this emissions category includes landfilling, composting, recycling, energy-from-waste processes, as well as wastewater treatment.

Business travel

This emissions category captures the GHG emissions associated with the transportation of employees for business-related activities, in vehicles owned or controlled by third parties.

An important distinction between this emissions category and that of mobile combustion is that the emissions captured within this category relate to transportation of employees in vehicles not owned or controlled by the reporting company, rather, they are owned or controlled by a third party. The GHG emissions associated with business travel might relate to road, sea, rail or air transportation and could be quantified through the collection of data regarding fuel consumption, distance travelled or alternatively through spend-based emissions factors.

Employee commuting

This emissions category captures the GHG emissions associated with the commuting of employees to and from the reporting company. These emissions might be associated with travel in personal vehicles, car-shares, commuting via public transport such as bus, rail or tube, air travel, as well as low-carbon travel such as walking or cycling. This emissions category can also be used to calculate the GHG emissions of those employees who do not commute owing to full-time remote working, as well as those who are part-time remote working.

Upstream leased assets

This emissions category captures the GHG emissions associated with leased assets and their operation. These assets should be leased and operated during the reporting year, and not already included within the inventory of Scope 1 or Scope 2 emissions categories. Examples of leased assets might be machinery, vehicles or building space.

Downstream transport and distribution

This emissions category captures the GHG emissions associated with the transport and distribution of products sold by the reporting company during the reporting year, in vehicles or facilities not owned or controlled by the reporting company. It is important to note that the emissions accounted for within this category only apply to those associated with the transport and distribution of products from the point of sale. The GHG emissions accounted for within this emissions category might be associated with air, rail, road and sea transport, as well as warehouses, distribution centres and retail facilities.

Processing of sold products

This emissions category captures the GHG emissions associated with the processing of sold intermediate products by third parties, following the sale by the reporting company. The GHG Protocol defines intermediate products as products that require further processing, transformation or inclusion in another product before use, and therefore result in the emission of GHGs from processing subsequent to sale by the reporting company and before use by the end consumer.

Use of sold products

This emissions category captures the GHG emissions associated with the use of goods or services which are sold by the reporting company during the reporting year. These emissions include the Scope 1 and Scope 2 emissions associated with the use of the sold product by the consumer. Companies are required to report on the direct use-phase emissions, which might encompass direct energy consumption during the use of a product, fuel and/or feedstock, or the GHGs that are emitted during the use of a product. It is optional for the reporting company to report on the indirect use-phase emissions, which includes products that indirectly consume energy or fuels during use.

The calculations that underpin the quantification of emissions relating to this emissions category often require design specifications or assumptions regarding the use of the product or service by the consumer across the estimated lifetime of the product.

End-of-life treatment of sold products

This emissions category captures the GHG emissions associated with the disposal and waste management of products sold by the reporting company, during the reporting year, at the end of the product lifespan. A company might calculate the GHG emissions associated with this emissions category by quantifying the total mass of sold products and packaging during the reporting year, in addition to a breakdown of the waste management processes used to dispose of this product waste at the end of life. Data regarding the waste-disposal behaviours of consumers within different regions can be difficult to obtain and might require some level of consumer research.

Downstream leased assets

This emissions category captures the GHG emissions associated with the operation of assets which are owned by the reporting company yet leased to another entity in the reporting year, and that are not included within Scope 1 or Scope 2.

Franchises

This emissions category captures the GHG emissions associated with the operation of any franchises of the reporting company, during the reporting year. When calculating the GHG emissions associated with this emissions category, the reporting company should account for GHG emissions associated with Scope 1 and Scope 2 emissions categories of the franchisee.

Investments

This emissions category captures the GHG emissions associated with investments made by the reporting company during the reporting year. This emissions category is only applicable to investors, companies providing financial services, as well as investors that are not profit driven. The GHG accounting approaches for this section differ depending on the financial investment or service of the reporting company.

It may appear unnecessarily bureaucratic and cumbersome but this level of guidance is totally necessary to enable one company to be compared to another, or even one year to another. Before the GHG Protocol it was like the Wild West in terms of environmental claims. Having a standardized approach to these things was essential, even if the language is a little dry.

How to design your product/service/process with less impact

Moving beyond carbon I want to now look at the practicalities and approaches to more environmentally conscious or regeneratively designed products.

Design is the single most powerful environmental tool there is. This is a big statement but I think it's true. I don't just mean the design of products, buildings, services, packaging and processes, I also mean the design of business models and the design of desire. Design can be used to make things last longer with less impact; design can be used to make you want more stuff, different stuff and better stuff; design can be used to make you happy with what you have already got. This section will focus on product design, packaging design and process design and will therefore help you think about how to make greater profit with less impact.

Product design

Applying sustainability to product design was initially driven by cost savings rather than sustainability and, as discussed previously, early product designers concentrated on designing in obsolescence rather than designing it out. Things have changed and that's partly a result of the desire to drive costs down and partly due to rising environmental awareness. I lecture on sustainable design in the UK at the University of Loughborough and the lecture is open to all industrial design students. This is increasingly normal now. Research that I undertook for the UK Design Council in 1997 indicated that at least 80 per cent of the environmental impact of a product is determined at the design stage (some is still dependent upon user habits but even these are influenced by design). Furthermore, other research by the Design Council at the same time indicated that time spent solving problems in the design phase was 100 times more cost effective than solving it at the production phase. It is therefore significantly cheaper to solve sustainability problems by designing them out at the beginning.

The way that I tackle this is to identify the largest environmental impact of the product first. For anything that uses energy this is likely to be energy during the use phase. For an oven, for example, ensuring greater insulation, a double-glazed (or even triple-glazed) door, an internal light so you don't need to open the door to check progress, and a sensor to shut-off the heat supply when opening the door are all sensible additions even if they increase raw material use a little.

Digging into the science here is exceptionally important. My guess is that you've begun to look at this already and you have a good understanding of where to focus your attention. Having said that, I do have one example of a company focusing on the wrong issues: a business that made appliances that use energy. The use of these appliances made up over half of their carbon impact, yet the appetite in the business was to focus on packaging reduction. This was erroneous in two ways. Firstly, it made up a fraction of 1 per cent of the environmental impact, and secondly, reducing packaging increases the likelihood of the product being damaged.

Generally available guidance about sustainable design throws up the same checklist from numerous sources. It goes something like this:

1 Choose non-toxic, sustainably produced or recycled materials which have a lower environmental impact than traditional materials.

2 Opt for manufacturing processes and produce products which are more energy efficient than traditional processes and end products.
3 Build longer-lasting and better-functioning products which will have to be replaced less frequently. This reduces the impact of producing replacements.
4 Design products for re-use and recycling. Make them easy to disassemble so that the parts can be re-used to make new products.
5 Consult sustainable design standards and guides.
6 Consider product life cycle. Use life cycle analysis tools to help you design more sustainable products.
7 Shift the consumption mode from personal ownership of products to provision of services which provide similar functions.
8 Materials should come from nearby, sustainably managed renewable sources that can be composted when their usefulness is exhausted.

Let's dig into these a little.

CHOOSE NON-TOXIC, SUSTAINABLY PRODUCED OR RECYCLED MATERIALS WHICH HAVE A LOWER ENVIRONMENTAL IMPACT THAN TRADITIONAL MATERIALS

This makes sense. Unless those alternative materials don't last as long or have no obvious waste treatment. An example here is compostable plastics. On the face of it they sound great, they just disappear. But in reality some (not all) won't last as long as non-compostable plastics. Others don't compost (I had a home-compostable bag from a UK supermarket chain in my domestic compost heap for over a year; it's probably still there). Furthermore, many countries do not have any waste infrastructure for compostable plastics and hence they will, at best, make their way to landfill or incineration, and at worst make it into the standard plastic recycling stream where they contaminate the stream, melt at a lower temperature and can result in damage to intrusion or extrusion machinery.

OPT FOR MANUFACTURING PROCESSES AND PRODUCE PRODUCTS WHICH ARE MORE ENERGY EFFICIENT THAN TRADITIONAL PROCESSES AND END PRODUCTS

Absolutely, this is good advice. It is sensible to make things as efficiently as you can and make efficient things. This is probably the number one consideration. We will look at process (manufacturing) design shortly.

BUILD LONGER-LASTING AND BETTER-FUNCTIONING PRODUCTS WHICH WILL HAVE TO BE REPLACED LESS FREQUENTLY, WHICH REDUCES THE IMPACT OF PRODUCING REPLACEMENTS

Longevity is definitely my favourite strategy in eco-design. Reducing the impact per use/wear or per year is a sensible strategy. To do this we need to understand what causes a product to fail, and design that component or element in a better way. There are many examples here that are interesting. The first was a client that I worked with in around 2006. They made large white goods, domestic appliances. In terms of product design we had some fun. I ran a day-long eco-design training session with 30 or so design engineers. I was warned that they would be a bit grumpy and hard to engage. So I took a brave approach. I stood on top of one of their washing machines to introduce myself and the concept of eco-design. We talked about the enabling factors that would allow for better eco-design. Given that washing temperature is a massive influencer of energy use it is impossible for a washing machine manufacturer to design a low temperature machine without the detergent manufacturers having a low temperature detergent. Furthermore the consumer also needs to trust that lower temperature washes work (I appreciate these are normal now but back then washing clothes in lukewarm water was not common). The key observation here is to widen your thinking from the product to the system in which it is being used. What would enable or constrain a better design approach?

I had their attention. I wasn't going to lecture them, I was going to work with them by stimulating their curiosity. I then jumped off the machine and took the top off. The top was made from virgin materials. Why? It could easily be made from recycled materials. So that's what they did. So too the soap drawer. Then I asked: What usually fails first on the machine? What do they get called out most for? Either under warranty or outside of warranty? The team quickly chirped up 'The main control board'. Brilliant, I said, why does it fail? 'Shorting from getting wet'. Great, I said. Where is it located in the machine? 'Under the main water inlet valve,' they replied.

You know what I said next don't you?

Shall we move it?

'Genius,' they replied. It may not have been genius, but it was a good idea. Let's think about this a little. If this board fails within the warranty period, the business has to send out an engineer to diagnose and replace it. That costs money. It is also a massive inconvenience for the owner. It has an environmental impact too. Not just the replacement part but the travel to and from the machine. Now, even worse, what if it fails outside of warranty? The owner would get a quote for a replacement part. These range from £90–190. Then there is the labour and travel. You are looking at around £300–400 for this repair. What's the cost of a new machine? You can get a brand new washing machine from the manufacturer in question for under £200. What would you do? Repair or replace? Most people would replace, unless they owned a more expensive machine.

I know what you're thinking. If things were made to last longer the wheels would fall off our business model. But not necessarily. Most car manufacturers now (not Tesla) make the majority of their profit from servicing rather than selling cars (Tesla will, in time, make most of theirs though the sale of renewable energy via their charging network). The days of sell it and forget it are long gone. With a depletion of retail margins (unless the manufacturer is able to sell direct), brands need to change the way they make profit and having a longer relationship with the customer is one such way. The aim here is to maximize the profitability per year of ownership rather than per unit sold. This way the customer sees an enhanced service for the money they pay, it becomes in the brand's interest to keep the product alive longer and those resources within the economy.

DESIGN PRODUCTS FOR RE-USE AND RECYCLING. MAKE THEM EASY TO DISASSEMBLE SO THAT THE PARTS CAN BE RE-USED TO MAKE NEW PRODUCTS

Again this makes sense, once we have designed them for longevity. There is a counter argument here, however. If the product is likely to have a short life (a fast fashion item or a single-use item like a vape) then totally focus on re-use or recycling. The fast fashion industry has embraced this in terms of chemical recycling and that makes sense for them. If they move all fabrics to polyester and close the loop by either reselling those items or recycling them (mechanically or chemically) then design for re-use and recycling trumps design for longevity. This is particularly important as businesses evolve from product businesses to service businesses. Keeping the components or the materials alive for longer really matters.

CONSULT SUSTAINABLE DESIGN STANDARDS AND GUIDES (E.G. DESIGN FOR THE ENVIRONMENT)

This is trickier than it sounds as one size does not fit all. I'd say the best thing to do is spend time with the customer to work out how the product will be used, talk to the 'waste' industry to look at the end-of-life and recycling realities, and develop the product and business model from this intelligence.

CONSIDER PRODUCT LIFE CYCLE. USE LIFE CYCLE ANALYSIS TOOLS TO HELP YOU DESIGN MORE SUSTAINABLE PRODUCTS

Life cycle analysis (LCA) is a method of calculating the environmental impact of a product from resource extraction, to product, use and disposal. There are very few free

LCA tools available. However OpenLCA is one such free-to-use tool. You will need the bill of materials for your product and you will need to understand where the individual components come from. This is no small undertaking but it will give you a good understanding of where in the life cycle the greatest impact is. However, you will probably get 80 per cent of the way with a good carbon footprint and some 'common sense'.

SHIFT THE CONSUMPTION MODE FROM PERSONAL OWNERSHIP OF PRODUCTS TO PROVISION OF SERVICES WHICH PROVIDE SIMILAR FUNCTIONS

I covered this early in the book and it is an increasingly important element of sustainability. I've long said that the real challenge in sustainable business is the business model. Making more or the same money from 'selling' less 'stuff' is the key challenge we face. Decoupling the buying of things from happiness and self-worth is an existential challenge worthy of a book all on its own, but this is crucial to the debate around sustainability. We are not what we buy or consume. We are what we do and how we make people feel. On the more palatable end of this debate is the shift from product to service as a core business model. I gave the example of denim jeans earlier. But this applies to many products. I worked with electronic components company RS Components to develop new business models aligned with the circular economy. One of the products they sold was a high-bay lighting system for warehouses. It was an LED system and there is a perception that LEDs don't get hot. They do and when they do a kind of cataract forms across then diminishing light output. Therefore, it is essential to have heat transfer away from the LEDs. Consequently, the lights had a huge chunk of aluminium as a heat sink and were therefore very expensive. They were also exceptionally efficient and we wanted them to 'sell' well. I mooted the idea of leasing the lights. The company weren't ready for that so we introduced a contract whereby the customer would buy the light but RS would give a guaranteed buy-back price that tapered over time. Did it sell? You bet. We saw an 8,000 per cent increase in sales. I'm going to type that again. We saw an 8,000 per cent increase in sales. Now some of this was down to the maturation of a new technology and the market waking up to it. But the sales team were adamant that the buy-back scheme was a key element to the success. This is interesting as we see the shift from purchasing to leasing as a binary choice. Whereas in reality there are nuanced business models that sit between the two.

MATERIALS SHOULD COME FROM NEARBY, SUSTAINABLY MANAGED RENEWABLE SOURCES THAT CAN BE COMPOSTED WHEN THEIR USEFULNESS IS EXHAUSTED

Well, this is a broad one. Let's break it down.

Materials should come from nearby sources: How important is this really? It actually depends on the weight of the material and its embedded impact. A heavy product with low embedded carbon impact is better sourced locally. A higher impact product that is light in weight and shipped by boat is totally different, transit is nearly irrelevant in terms of its proportional impact. I spoke at an event on sustainability and there was a very high profile handbag designer there who said how massively important local supply was. In reality, for a leather bag, the distance pales into insignificance beside the embedded impact of a leather bag.

Sustainably managed renewable resources: Absolutely. The only challenge here is the legitimacy of the accreditation body for sustainable supply. It is increasingly important to the customer to be able to justify and defend the sustainability of their products. Consequently there are many certifications relating to the sustainability of resource supply. These include generic certifications (see the specific section of certifications) but of most interest here are the material-specific certifications that offer a greater level of granularity and a more in-depth assessment of raw material and resource sustainability. There are so many of these and they cover a wide range of resources including:

· wood and timber
· paper fibres
· organic food
· palm oil
· latex
· textile yarns
· leather
· coffee
· tea

And many more. Each one will charge a small fee to use their logo and to check your claims (or your supplier's claims). Some are well known by the public and some less so. The advent of blockchain has the potential to open up supply chains to greater visibility. This is to be welcomed.

That can be composted when their usefulness is exhausted: This is a rather unusual one. For food waste and fabric this makes sense. But as soon as we step into the world of compostable plastics this becomes less meaningful. These plastics take a considerable amount of time to compost (way longer than claimed in many cases) and often (despite being 'approved' for home composting) require higher temperatures than are reached in a home compost heap. I have a very unfashionable view: I'd rather use traditional plastics that can be recovered and recycled, that are circular in the technological cycle rather than lost into compost. The energy required to grow, harvest, process and form bioplastics is in line with that embedded (yep including oil extraction) within normal plastics. My view is that embedded impact is best kept embedded in the resource and used again. Additionally, there is a lively debate regarding whether it is best to use land to grow food or plastics. The crops that are used to produce the chemicals required to make compostable and bio-plastics can also be eaten. There are some interesting developments in this space, however: PlantBottle (created by Coca-Cola) is a bottle that is a combination of plant materials (from sugars) and oil-based materials to produce a PET (polyethylene terephthalate) bottle with less non-renewable resources but that can be recycled with 'normal' PET. The reason that this is interesting is that it isn't composted; the chemistry, the value, is kept cycling.

Looking beyond these approaches the design industry talks in terms of design for sustainability and there are a number of approaches that are broadly followed:

A – Design for long life

This is a really simple approach. Design products that last a long time. This means that their impact per wear/use/year is reduced. The challenges here are around purchase price and business model.

B – Design for short life

What? Really? Yep, there is some logic here. Those products that have a short lives in terms of use (packaging, fast fashion, exhibition stands and exhibition furniture) could be designed for short life. Way back in 2002 we exhibited at a large sustainability show in the UK. We used cardboard furniture so that it could be recycled at the end of life rather than thrown away. Some stand furniture is stored but this takes up space. We actually stored our cardboard furniture (it folded flat) and used it for 10 years. The interesting thing is that we got more enquiries about the furniture than we did our carbon footprinting and environmental strategy services. We were clearly too early.

C – Design for dematerialization

Wow, fancy. Well, a fancy way of saying lean design. Can we design our products and packaging with as few components as possible? As few fixings as possible? Can we apply lean thinking to product and packaging design? Of course we can and we sometimes do. I've made a career out of asking 'why'. Why is that component there? Why do you assemble it in three parts when you could do it in two? Why do you have speed humps on the HGV road in? (This was a fascinating one: a large homeware giant found that the bottom row of pots on each pallet sent to stores were broken. They considered increasing packaging. I watched the lorries get loaded and leave. I watched them crunch down as they went over the speed humps. I checked the pots as they were loaded and when they reached the end of the driveway. They were broken on the driveway. The speed humps were exceptionally aggressive, so we smoothed them. Problem solved.) Why does that fruit machine need two gas struts to hold up the front when one will do? Why build the foaming soap pump into each pack when it could be in the dispenser?

I appreciate that not all of these are about dematerialization, some are about process, but the same principle applies. Ask why something is designed the way it is. Often you will get the response 'we've always done it like that'. That's a sign, a sign that things need to change. Can you design the product, pack, service or process to give the same utility with less materials, layers or stages? Can you do so without reducing the length of life or amount of joy? Then do it.

D – Design for energy efficiency

If the product or service you sell uses energy then how can you design it to use less? Clearly energy use in the use phase is a big issue and in the EU we have seen the advent and relatively easy adoption of energy efficiency labels for most kitchen appliances and for light bulbs; in the United States the Energy Star label has enhanced energy efficiency. The advent of the EU system has been estimated to have saved 230 million tonnes of oil (by 2030) and $290 a year per household. If efficiency can be improved through design then the end user has an easier job of reducing their impact.

E – Design for chemical safety

The advent of chemicals legislation and extended producer responsibility has changed the requirements upon manufacturers to ensure products are safe in the European Union. Many US states have similar legislation and other countries are following suit. Long gone are the days when chemicals were liberally added to products. We still see high chemical use in clothing, especially in cotton. This is a concern not just for our health but for the health of the wider ecosystem as some of these chemicals (known as 'forever chemicals') don't break down over time. They literally stay in our ecosystems forever. The chemicals known as polyfluoroalkyl substances are a family of about 10,000 chemicals that are valued for their non-stick and detergent properties. They have been found in water, soils and sediments. They have been found in 17,000 sites across the UK and are widespread in nearly all of the Global North. They are used in a wide range of consumer products and waste and industrial processes. They are used in non-stick cookware, water-repellent clothing, stain resistant fabrics and carpets, some cosmetics, some firefighting foams and products that resist grease, water and oil.

F – Design for circularity

As discussed previously there are numerous strategies to enhance circularity. You need to choose the one that is most relevant and appropriate for the product and the customer/user. This may be design for re-use, refurbishment, service, leave, recovery and recycling, or longevity.

In essence developing an appropriate eco-design or design for sustainability strategy necessitates understanding the largest impact of your product throughout its life cycle and focusing on this; understanding the way the product is used and disposed of, and how it is misused. These elements will then determine your design approach. They need to be accompanied by some form of user advice regarding product use-phase impacts. Simple things like turning the oven down between cooking pizzas, hitting standby or off on your PC at the end of the day, washing at lower temperatures, how to recycle your packaging. The challenge here is informing the consumer without preaching.

That's all well and good; you've redesigned your product. Now you just need to make it.

How to develop a lower impact manufacturing process

It is increasingly likely that, if you make a physical product, it will be made overseas. Although we are seeing some re-shoring of manufacture the manufacturing nations of the world are China (most goods), India, Pakistan, Morocco, Bangladesh, Vietnam and Cambodia (clothing and shoes), China and Taiwan (electronics). This doesn't matter. It is sensible to apply process-efficient design regardless of where the manufacturing base is. Indeed the carbon impact of electricity in many manufacturing countries is higher than in the Global North and West as it is (at the moment but not for long) predominantly coal-derived.

The sustainability world and the lean-manufacturing world overlap at this point.

What is lean manufacturing?

It is a production philosophy that aims to maximize value while minimizing waste in order to boost productivity and efficiency. It is a systematic form of production that aims to decrease waste, reorganize workflows and cut costs. This means that it also (in every case I've applied it) reduces environmental impact too. Lean manufacturing is a concept that was first introduced in Japan in the 1950s and has subsequently been adopted by many manufacturers and has become an essential element of contemporary production.

Lean manufacturing's fundamental goal is to find and get rid of waste in all areas of the production process. In this context we widen the definition of waste to refer to any process or action that does not improve the ultimate good or service. Lean manufacturing aims to remove the following seven categories of waste:

1 **Over-production:** Producing more than is required by the customer, resulting in excess inventory and unnecessary costs. This clearly has an environmental impact also.
2 **Waiting:** Delays in the production process due to idle time, machine breakdowns or waiting for materials or information. Once again, having manufacturing equipment left on and not producing product results in increased environmental impact.

3 **Transportation:** Moving materials, products or equipment unnecessarily, resulting in increased costs and potential damage. Both of which have an environmental impact.

4 **Processing:** Using more resources than necessary to produce a product, resulting in increased costs and reduced efficiency. Any unnecessary processing results in greater environmental impact.

5 **Inventory:** Excess inventory of raw materials, work in progress or finished goods, resulting in increased costs and potential waste. Believe it or not this produces an environmental impact too. If you are holding significant quantities of stock and the market changes or technology changes there is a risk of product not being sold and therefore being scrapped, or having to be sold at a reduced price and therefore reducing margins.

6 **Motion:** Unnecessary movement of people or equipment, resulting in wasted time and energy. This is a big one. Henry Ford tackled this back in the early 20th century. Moving people around a factory was less efficient than moving the car around the factory, hence the introduction of production lines. I still see unnecessary movement of people or product when I visit a factory now. The environmental impact is less obvious in this case.

7 **Defects:** Producing products or services that do not meet customer requirements, resulting in rework, scrap and potential damage to the company's reputation. Once more, a clear environmental and cost implication.

Through applying lean manufacturing techniques several kinds of waste are eliminated, efficiency is improved and productivity is raised. One approach that is shared with waste minimization methodologies is value stream mapping. This entails examining the entire manufacturing process to spot waste and inefficiencies. This study is used to create a plan for streamlining processes and removing waste to improve the process.

Standardized work processes are another essential component in lean manufacturing. For this, each task in the production process must be divided into smaller, easier-to-manage phases, and each step must then have regular work instructions. This lessens the possibility of mistakes or flaws while also assisting in ensuring uniformity and quality throughout the production process.

Another important concept in lean manufacturing is the use of a pull-based production system. This means that production is driven by customer demand, with products or services only being produced when they are needed. This helps to reduce inventory and waste and ensures that resources are used efficiently.

Lean manufacturing also places a big emphasis on continuous improvement. This entails continuously evaluating and analysing the manufacturing process in order to spot areas for improvement and introducing new procedures to boost productivity and cut waste. With the intention of fostering a culture of constant innovation and development, continuous improvement is accomplished through a process of experimentation and learning.

Lean manufacturing is a potent manufacturing, cost and sustainability philosophy that can aid you in boosting productivity, cutting waste, enhancing quality and reducing environmental impact. It will help drive sustainable profits.

The overlaps between lean manufacturing and waste minimization in the production process are significant. In my early career from 1994 to 1999 I saw two or three different businesses a week. For each one I drew a process flow diagram to understand not only where the waste was produced during the process, but also to understand where the value was added.

Modern manufacturing procedures place a strong emphasis on minimizing waste with the main objective of minimizing costs and environmental impact. It is a thorough approach to waste management that includes locating waste sources, calculating and evaluating waste creation (this isn't just physical waste, it also includes seconds, rework, waste heat and light, amongst other things), putting waste minimization techniques into practice and assessing the success of those efforts. We shall examine the main facets of waste minimization in manufacturing and then I will demonstrate with a simple process flow diagram (Figure 8.1).

IDENTIFYING SOURCES OF WASTE

Finding the waste sources in the manufacturing process is the first step in applying waste minimization. An evaluation of the production process, including the usage of raw materials, energy utilization and waste disposal, can help to achieve this. Every apparatus and equipment that may help generate waste should be considered in the assessment. I find it really useful to draw this out. For each process I draw the inputs and the outputs (see Figure 8.1).

FIGURE 8.1   Example of a process flow diagram

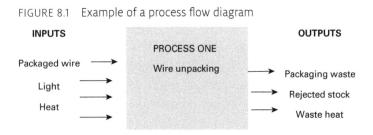

Once you've detailed all the inputs and outputs you need to calculate the costs per unit (per kg steel wire, per kWh of power and per hour of labour) then add these in. Do the same with the outputs. Cost per kg of waste, value of rejected stock (not just the materials value, also factor in the wasted time to sort, operate and process this) and apply a percentage of the cost and impact associated with light and heat. As you move further through the process you can add a cost per kg of product at that stage of the process. For nails the main processes that add value are the wire formation, cutting to length, point trimming and head forming. Reducing waste all along the process is essential but particularly towards the end of the process where most of the value will have been added to the product.

ANALYSING AND MEASURING WASTE PRODUCTION

The next stage is to measure and analyse the amount of waste produced by the production process at each stage. As previously mentioned, this needs to assessed in terms of weight/volume (this can then be converted to carbon) and also in terms of money. What I would be particularly interested in here is why is this waste occurring? Are the raw materials out of specification? Is there an issue with damage on delivery? Have they been damaged on arrival or in processing?

How much is this costing you? It is really important to get to the reasons that sit behind waste. This also applies to service businesses that don't make a product. Restaurants and bars for example also have significant levels of waste and mapping the processes used here is essential to reducing impact.

One of my contracts was to support the NHS on waste reduction. I worked on two sub-projects. One looking at the waste arising from a knee operation and one from the catering side of the organization. The savings identified were massive, something in the region of £5 million per year from one knee procedure and the patient meals service in one hospital. On the meals service side, the process was full of challenges. Patients ordered off a lunch menu but they ordered the day before. Those orders were cooked straight after breakfast. Therefore lunch was ready by 10.30 and kept warm in massive aluminium trays. When lunch was served between 12.00 and 14.00 how do you think that lunch tasted? Yep, pretty shite. Guess what proportion of the meals were eaten? Fifty-five per cent. The things that were more often left were the vegetables. Now, we can argue whether or not food is medicine but one thing is for sure, not eating a wide and balanced diet is clearly unhealthy. Yet our sickest people were being served stale food with all the nutrients cooked out of it. And don't get me started on the offer in the cafeteria. All I did was look at the waste arising after each meal. I always start in the bins. The bins show you very quickly what is wrong with a business. All the dirty secrets are here to see. I worked with one large wholesaler and I started in the bins. In one 1,100 litre wheeled bin I found over £8,000 of stock. None of it broken or damaged. I asked why. Well, they said. Anything that's returned after ordering, used or not, faulty or not, that has a value of less than £200 is just binned. We soon changed that. We worked out the cost of reprocessing and stocking returns and lowered this threshold to £25. Problem solved, extra income guaranteed. I looked in the other bins and the average value returned (due the customer changing their mind mainly) was £6,000. There were tens of bins. Always start in the trash.

IMPLEMENTING STRATEGIES TO MINIMIZE WASTE GENERATION

Waste minimization is the aim of this game. Therefore establishing strategies to do so builds on lean approaches to manufacturing. Among the most successful approaches are:

1 **Process optimization:** This is the process of making manufacturing procedures more efficient in order to produce less waste. Process control systems, equipment changes and lean manufacturing techniques can all help with this.

2 **Material substitution:** The replacement of raw materials with less harmful substitutes. This can be done by sourcing goods from environmentally conscious sources or by using repurposed materials.

3 **Waste reduction and recycling:** Identifying why waste is generated and removing it at source is the most beneficial approach. But then look at the diversion of waste from landfill and into something more regenerative such as refurbishment, reprocessing and finally recycling.

4 **Pollution prevention:** The implementation of pollution prevention measures to minimize the impact of manufacturing processes on the environment. This can be achieved through the implementation of best practices, such as the use of pollution prevention technologies, and the implementation of environmental management systems.

MONITORING THE EFFECTIVENESS OF WASTE MINIMIZATION

Finally, it is critical to monitor the effectiveness of waste minimization efforts to ensure that they are achieving the desired results. This can be done through the implementation of KPIs and the regular review of waste management practices. The KPIs can be used to track progress towards waste minimization targets, and the review of waste management practices can be used to identify areas where improvements can be made.

The benefits of waste minimization in manufacturing are numerous. They include reduced operating costs, improved environmental performance, increased efficiency and reduced regulatory compliance costs. Waste minimization can also improve the reputation of the company by demonstrating a commitment to environmental sustainability, and it can help to attract and retain customers who value sustainable business practices.

One of the most significant challenges in waste minimization in manufacturing can be the cost of implementation. While the benefits of waste minimization are clear – as I have already said, I have saved my clients more than they have ever paid out – the upfront costs of implementing some waste minimization strategies can be substantial if they involve capital investment.

However, it is important to recognize that the cost of doing nothing can be far greater. The costs of non-compliance with environmental regulations, damage to the environment and damage to the company's reputation are unlimited. There are no profits to be made on a dead planet.

In conclusion, waste minimization is a critical aspect of modern manufacturing practices. It sits hand-in-glove with lean manufacturing and requires the same tenacity and skill set.

How to talk about environmental claims

The word 'greenwashing' has become common parlance over the last 20 years as businesses try and keep up with changing consumer demands and preferences for more sustainable products and services. It implies that the environmental claims relating to the product or service are over-hyped, distracting from the real impact of the product or are marketing words with little or no substance. It is when the organization spends more time making itself look green than being green. Well, there's a couple of new kids on the block in terms of terminology relating to environmental claims.

The first was coined by my friend Clare Potter. Clare works in eco-design and her observation was that many companies (and if I'm honest I see this more with individuals) have moved beyond greenwashing and into greencocking. It's a portmanteau of greenwashing and peacocking. So essentially leading with how great you are on sustainability, but probably only leading with one aspect of that performance or behaviour. I'm not necessarily saying that this is intended to obfuscate but it is more than misleading and underlines a trend that has been evident since my time working in a large UK supermarket which has gathered pace recently. This is the rush of marketing and brand to the sustainability 'space'. I can't tell you the amount of agencies that now offer sustainability advice or a 'blended' service, yet they do so without any environmental or scientific knowledge. The mantra 'never let the truth get in the way of a good story' springs to mind here.

My time with a leading UK supermarket was fascinating. I was the Environmental Manager (there was just one person looking after sustainability, but this was back in 1999/2000) and I was placed in the PR Team (or the PR Machine as they named themselves). The aim of the team was to get good stories in the paper, rather than to deliver great initiatives. So success was measured in column inches and public reaction rather than carbon. We still see this now. There is a much-heralded project with a fast-food chain that stopped giving kids toys with kids meals (forget the sustainability element, this was always lacking in morals). They took all those toys and reprocessed them to make trays for the stores. Great. A nice idea. But a tiny idea. The chain sells meat. They have a massive environmental footprint from that alone (and I mean massive), then they have stores in every large town on the planet. Then they have a supply chain that has (in the past) been related to removal of biodiversity and carbon sinks in order to graze animals. Now, I know for a fact that they are working on truly transformational improvements and changes to the very nature of their business; this is to be applauded. But all we hear about is toys and trays. Greencocking. It is exacerbated by the agencies and enablers that helped them – it is in their interest to shout about this. Always follow the money.

I'll put it as simply as I can: We do not have time to mess about with toys and trays; we need to halve carbon impact and do it fast. We need to look at the biggest impact of our businesses and go there. Messing about with the fripperies of our business is simply not enough. I sit writing this bit of the book the day after the UN released their survival guide to avert climate disaster and it has already fallen off the front pages of the online news sites. The report states that we will miss the 1.5°C warming limit. I know this, I have been saying it for years. We are guilty of talking and not doing. We are fractured in our environmental efforts, we have been divided and pitted against ourselves as an environmental movement and we have fallen for it. Time to come together, stop polishing that turd and start taking action. Business, enterprise, entrepreneurship have the power to solve these problems but only if we pull sustainability rather than green marketing into the centre of everything we do.

The second new phrase is 'green-hushing'. This is when a company stays silent on their carbon plans, their science-based net zero emissions targets. It's not that they don't have them, they do. They are just staying silent, predominantly to avoid accusations of greenwashing in the light of increased activity from, amongst others, the UK's Advertising Standards Authority (ASA). In the absence of regulatory control from other elements of government, the ASA have taken on a policing role that has stopped many campaigns already. Sometimes for valid reasons, sometimes these are a bit pedantic. But the implication is huge: companies are staying quiet.

So how do we talk about environmental and sustainability issues? Well, let's start with the guidance produced by the aforementioned ASA/Committee of Advertising Practice. The guidance is thorough and truly worth reading. In summary:

Always avoid using phrases like 'carbon neutral' or 'net zero' that are not supported by evidence. Advertisers should explain the reasoning behind these statements whenever they are made so that customers can comprehend them fully.

When making claims about carbon offsetting, marketing materials should provide factual information (i.e. the degree to which they are reducing carbon emissions). This will assist in preventing consumers from being duped or bamboozled into thinking certain goods or services don't emit any emissions.

Any future aspirational statements (such going net zero or being carbon neutral) must be supported by a strategy of delivery that can be independently verified.

Advertisers must also include information on the carbon offsetting programme they are using, and any statements regarding carbon offsetting must adhere to standards of evidence.

Where claims include qualifying information this must be easy to see and understand before customers make a purchase decision.

Absolute environmental assertions must be backed up by a sufficient amount of substantiation. The ASA has previously cited phrases like 'the greenest stoves on earth', 'save CO_2 emissions', 'plastic-free', '100% recyclable', 'widely recycled' and 'environmentally friendly' as examples of 'absolute environmental claims'. Any absolute assertions must be qualified by fact.

When there are conflicting scientific viewpoints or ambiguous evidence, it should be made plain to consumers what level of proof is necessary.

Regarding 'green advertising', further considerations for advertisers include the fact that comparative environmental claims – such as 'greener' or 'friendlier' – will need to be supported by data demonstrating that the product or service benefits the environment more than alternatives. This information should be mentioned in the advertisement, or it must be made abundantly obvious to customers where to find it.

Marketers must also make sure that any generic claims cover the whole life cycle of the product, from manufacturing to disposal (unless expressly qualified). 'Good for the world', 'helping to support a more sustainable future', '100% eco-friendly', 'good for the land', 'environmentally friendly', 'zero emissions', 'gives back to the environment' and 'less plastic' are a few examples of whole life cycle statements.

Marketers may make an environmental claim that solely applies to a portion of the life cycle of a service or product, but this should be stated explicitly.

In the case of an electric automobile, for instance, a claim of zero emissions might be allowed if the advertisement makes it clear that this solely applies to driving.

Importantly, marketing must not mislead customers about how an item or service will assist the environment.

There will be significant attention directed at all sustainability claims and businesses need to be water-tight in terms of the claim itself and the data used to back it up. The reputational damage of being prosecuted by the ASA will outweigh any potential benefit of telling your customers what you have done. This external pressure has quietened numerous companies who have undertaken significant and positive action to reduce their environmental footprint. However, the motivation behind a greater degree of scrutiny has been missing for decades and hence sustainability has often formed part of the marketing function. Not only is this erroneous, it is actually damaging, as marketing has historically been less interested in facts and more interested in noise. Those days are gone. Thankfully.

How to set science-based targets

What are science-based targets? The Science Based Targets Initiative outlines, defines and promotes best practice in carbon emissions reductions and net-zero targets in line with the best available science. These are goals that an organization sets to minimize its carbon footprint and are known as science-based carbon targets. They are geared towards hitting the Paris Agreement's stated goal of keeping global warming to 1.5°C over pre-industrial levels. Although, as we have already heard, this is now considered unlikely.

In order to develop science-based targets an organization should follow these outline processes:

1 *Understand your baseline emissions:* Understanding your baseline emissions is essential to reducing them. In order to do this, you must determine the overall amount of GHG emissions for which the company is accountable, including both direct emissions from internal activities and indirect emissions from external sources. See earlier in this chapter on how to undertake a Scope 1, 2 and 3 assessment.

2 *Undertake a sector baseline review if the relevant data is available:* Who is doing what and how? Where do you fit relative to your sector? What are the main sector challenges in terms of carbon? Are they structural challenges (no low-carbon alternative fuels, for example)? Are you seeing trends emerge here?

3 *Define the scope of the target:* The next step is to define the scope of the target. This involves determining which emissions sources the target will cover, such as Scope 1 and 2 alone or including Scope 3 also.

4 *Identify reduction opportunities:* Once the baseline emissions have been established, the organization should identify opportunities for reducing emissions. This can be achieved by conducting a carbon footprint analysis to determine the sources of emissions and identifying ways to reduce them. This element is often overlooked and is wedded to cost savings so is a sensible thing to spend some time on.

5 *Set reduction goals:* Based on the reduction opportunities identified in the previous step, the organization should

set goals for reducing emissions. These goals should be ambitious but achievable and should be based on the latest climate science.

6 *Engage stakeholders:* Engaging stakeholders is an essential step in developing a science-based targets approach. This involves consulting with employees, customers, suppliers and other stakeholders to ensure that the target is achievable and aligned with their expectations. Targets are easier to hit when everyone understands them and is working towards them. Your team will deliver your targets.

7 *Monitor progress:* Setting the target is just the start. The organization should now monitor its progress regularly to ensure that it remains on track to achieve its goals. This can be achieved by tracking emissions data, conducting regular carbon footprint analyses and reporting on progress to stakeholders.

There is a simple step-by-step guide for submitting your targets including a streamlined approach for small and medium-sized enterprises at sciencebasedtargets.org.

Remember to give yourself plenty of time. This is urgent but it is more of a marathon than a sprint. It is not a PR exercise. The aim is to be realistic, honest and at the same time ambitious.

How to sequester well

First off, what is sequestration? One method used to combat climate change is carbon sequestration. This involves extracting carbon from the atmosphere and storing it. There are two main types of sequestration. Geological and biological.

Geological

This is literally trapping carbon dioxide underground, and is known as carbon capture and storage. Carbon dioxide produced by industrial processes is piped or shipped to locations for deep underground storage in geological formations, ironically in deplete gas or oil fields, for example.

Creeping into this category is also graphene production. Graphene uses carbon dioxide as a raw material. Demand for graphene is expected to increase by a compound 46.6 per cent from 2023 to 2030.[1]

Biological

We are probably more aware of the biological sequestration options and approaches. The main options here are:

1 **Woodlands and forests:** Woodlands and forests are regarded as one of the best natural carbon sequestration methods. During photosynthesis, CO_2 binds to plants as part of photosynthesis and exchanges it for oxygen. It is estimated that forests store twice as much carbon as they emit. Protecting what we have (the biggest rainforest we have is in Brazil but the highest quality rainforest is in the Democratic Republic of the Congo) is essential. But not just the big forests; temperate rainforests, savannah, prairie, peat bogs and other natural environments also do a great job and require protection, not just as a carbon sink but as a source of biodiversity.

2 **Soil:** Soil is a great store for carbon. Not just the aforementioned peat bogs but also normal soil, agricultural soil. We have utterly failed to protect our soils and, indeed, modern farming methods lead to the loss of organic matter and therefore carbon from all farmed soils. If managed effectively the Massachusetts Institute of Technology estimate that soils (mainly agricultural soils) could sequester an additional billion tonnes of carbon each year.[2]

3 **Oceans:** Aquatic environments including large bodies of water are also great absorbers of CO_2. They absorb something approaching a quarter of emitted CO_2 from the earth's atmosphere. This carbon is mostly held in the upper layers of the oceans. When there is too much carbon held in water the acidity levels of the water rise and this makes carbonate ions less available. These ions are the building blocks to much sea life, from oyster shells, to some plankton, to, of course, coral reefs. It poses a significant threat to ocean health and stability undermining the entire food web. However, sea grass offers great potential for carbon sequestration as the carbon is stored in the plant and root zone.

Other forms of sequestration

The world of sequestration is getting simultaneously really exciting and attracting a great deal of scepticism. We are seeing the development of exciting techniques such as advanced weathering.

Advanced weathering for sequestration is a promising new carbon capture and storage method that involves accelerating the weathering of certain types of rocks to capture and store atmospheric carbon dioxide (CO_2). This naturally occurring process usually takes over millions of years but can be greatly accelerated by using new technologies to break the rocks down into small pieces, greatly increasing the rate of weathering and therefore the amount of carbon that can be stored.

The basic concept of advanced weathering is relatively simple. Certain types of rock, such as basalt, have the ability to react with CO_2 to form stable carbonates, effectively removing the gas from the atmosphere and storing it in solid form.

This process has several advantages over traditional carbon capture and storage processes. First, it is much less environmentally damaging as it is a natural process that requires no energy or chemicals. Second, it is a highly effective method of removing CO_2 from the atmosphere, with some estimates suggesting it could sequester 2 billion tonnes of CO_2 each year.[3]

Finally, it is relatively inexpensive (estimates vary from $80–180 per tonne of CO_2e removal) compared to other carbon capture and storage methods, making it an attractive option for countries and companies looking to reduce their carbon footprint.

However, there are also some challenges associated with advanced weathering. The main issue is the availability of rock suitable for the process. Basalt is one of the most effective rock types for weathering, but it is relatively rare and can be difficult to extract and transport.

Despite this, many researchers and companies are actively working to develop advanced weathering technologies and extend the process for commercial use. If successful, this could represent a major breakthrough in the fight against climate change and provide a safe, natural and inexpensive way to remove CO_2 from the atmosphere and store it for the long term.

Sequestration is easy to criticize. It is akin to doing as much harm as you like and then paying your way out of trouble rather than trying to reduce the impact of your operations. I get that. It is a fair criticism and not helped by the way that organizations talk about it: declaring themselves carbon neutral or net zero without explaining the length of time that sequestration takes, the types of sequestration invested in and then the action they will take to reduce their core footprint. Scandals in the verified offsetting schemes over the last two years have destroyed confidence in the sector, however sequestration has a crucial role to play in reducing carbon impact. Let me rephrase that: quality sequestration has a vital role to play. It will take a massive effort from everyone on Earth to stop the atmosphere from warming any further than it already has. Every viable answer, from reducing our reliance on carbon-emitting fuels to setting a net zero emissions target by 2050, is critical if we are to avert unprecedented climate change.

Humanity is working diligently to reduce carbon emissions by changing the way we build, consume and travel, as well as switching to clean energy sources and decarbonizing high-emission activities like construction and transportation. Sequestration is not a silver bullet but it is part of the solution.

How to train your team

Your team are the key to bringing this to life and keeping it alive. Not only should they be involved in developing and establishing the policy and strategy but they are the people who will:

- have the most contact with your customers so will have the greatest understanding of their desires and needs
- have the greatest contact with suppliers so will understand the supply-chain opportunities best
- be the closest to the product or service so will have a greater understanding of how to enhance or improve it from a sustainability perspective

A good first step here is to book in some carbon literacy training via carbonliteracy.com (run by the Carbon Literacy Trust). Then either buy in or develop specific training that relates to your industry. There are many free resources online and you can also talk to your local authority as there may be support available. Other great sources of training and training materials include your trade association who will have developed and delivered training that pertains to your industry and industry sector. Alternatively there are many private-sector trainers who can help you and you may be able to pull some training together yourself. Use training as an opportunity to harness ideas and champion great work.

Building a better business: A checklist

1 Start with your purpose. What is your 'why'?

....
....
....
....

2 Undertake a simple carbon footprint.

....
....
....
....

3 Develop an environmental policy – give it some personality.

....
....
....
....

4 Develop your environmental strategy. Remember to talk to the team and your customers.

....
....
....
....

5   Strategy is great but building a culture counts. Have you worked on building a culture of curiosity and sustainability? What could you do to make this easier and better?

....
....
....
....

6   Consider Scope 1 and 2 carbon assessments.

....
....
....
....

7   What about Scope 3?

....
....
....
....

8   How can you use design (product design, packaging design or process design) to design impact out?

....
....
....
....

9   Do you want to go public with your environmental claims? If so what is the best way of doing this? It needs to be authentic and science-based.

....

....

....

....

10 Do you want to sequester (offset) your impact? If so how and who with?

....

....

....

....

11 What training do you need to undertake?

....

....

....

....

CHAPTER NINE

Re-framing business

If business does anything well, that thing is change.

It is able to respond to changing circumstances, shifting markets, changes in consumer preference and legislation. It applies creativity successfully to nearly every aspect of its practices, from tax to product innovation. Why hasn't it, then, applied creativity effectively to the environmental and sustainability challenges we face?

I covered this early in the book and it is almost entirely down to the success measures we place on business. Namely profit. However, as we have learnt, profit is too one-dimensional a measure of success. Indeed, the sole and relentless pursuit of financial profit is the fastest way to damage and destroy environmental value. Traditional cultures, including many in the Global West, have understood this and worked to ensure that future generations can still thrive. We lost this when we lost our connection to nature. The conversion of raw materials to money ignores the source of real wealth.

I've said it many times, and it has inspired the title of this book: while business is the cause of most of the environmental problems we face, enterprise is probably the only thing that can solve these problems. And it is this natural creativity within business that needs to be harnessed.

What is creativity?

Creativity is defined in many ways. But definitions don't help much. They've pushed us towards seeing creativity as a skill monopolized by a small subset of people. The stereotypical image of a creative person is someone who probably dresses one standard deviation from the normal, probably wears funky glasses and defines themselves as 'A Creative', as if it's a proper noun. Indeed some brands target their services or their products at 'the creative man or woman'. I know a jeans company that do this. If you've got legs you can wear jeans, and if you've got a brain then you're creative.

My definition of creativity is this:

> Creativity is simply imagining a world that hasn't arrived yet.

It doesn't mean that you have to be able to sketch, write, paint, CAD, photograph or film that vision. They are all amazing ways that we can bring creativity to life. But the act of creativity is one of imagination.

So if creativity is imagining a world that hasn't arrived yet why would we imagine a worse one? One of the challenges with sustainability, and in particular communicating sustainability, is that we focus on the negative. It is easy to slip into the mindset of shock and fear. Focusing on catastrophizing the challenges that we face is a natural way of encouraging people to care. But it has, demonstrably, not worked. What we have missed in this whole debate is the strength, the benefits, the incentive of imagining a world that is better in every way; that is fairer in every way. In that world there is no place for industry or practices that damage the natural resource base and biodiversity or threaten to use resources at an unsustainable rate, unless there are other resources already in view.

But sadly, business is too focused on the short term. I'd go further and say that policy and governance is too focused on the short term also. With most democratic systems having four- or five-year election cycles there is a lack of long-term thinking. Organizations like the OECD and the UN can think beyond these time frames (I acknowledge that both of these organizations have limitations, bias and their fair share of challenges), however, there aren't many organizations that can sit above national governments and think more strategically.

The OECD, in a recent report, highlighted the shortcomings of short-term policy thinking.[1] Fiscally there are many, let alone environmentally. For example the financial impacts of wild fire suppression, crop insurance, air quality associated healthcare and coastal disaster relief (please note this is a very limited range of climate change impacts) are likely to rise (median figures used) by 300 per cent and could rise by 1,000 per cent between the middle of this century and the end. Yet, and this is the point I want to make, the Long-Term Budget Outlook of US Congress does not discuss climate change or the policy direction required to mitigate its impacts.

The EU is a little more creative when it comes to its policy approach (yes policy needs to be creative too as policy is the mechanism through which we can achieve the better world that we have imagined). The EU reported in 2020 on the likely areas of public spending impacted by climate change. These are split into non-discretionary (driven by climate change) and discretionary (driven by policy measures).

Non-discretionary impacts on public spending

Direct impacts that are likely to increase public expenditure in this area include: repair or replacement of infrastructure and buildings; social transfers to households affected by weather events; financing of explicit contingent liabilities (for example state guarantees for insurance schemes).

Indirect impacts that are likely to increase public expenditure in this area include: reduction of tax revenues due to reductions in economic activity; increase in social welfare payments due to reductions in economic activity; materialization of implicit contingent liabilities (for example to support financial institutions in distress); impact of sovereign capacity to meet debt repayments due to funds reallocation towards climate change.

Discretionary impact through policy measure spending

There will be spending on adaptation measures, including:

- public investment in climate-proofing infrastructure and protecting water supply;
- subsidies to support farmers to change crop varieties and methods;
- subsidies to assist relocation of populations from coastal or other flood-prone areas.

There will also be increased spending required for mitigation policies. This is a Pandora's Box of guesses as there are so many unknowns and many risks that are yet to become clear. But, for example, carbon taxes on fossil fuels are likely to have an immediate adverse impact on income and unknown longer-term impacts. For example, the shift to electric car fleets and the development of renewable energy supplies (both of which often attract lower taxation rates than fossil fuels and internal combustion powered vehicles) will see tax revenues fall. However, it is significantly more complex than this as nearly all governments subsidize (either directly or via significant taxation breaks) the fossil fuel industry. These are complex balances of expenditure and receipts, although this one is likely to reduce public expenditure due to: emissions trading scheme revenues; subsidies for clean energy transition; redistribution impacts upon the tax base.

My point is not to create an exhaustive list, rather it is to underline the folly of leaving climate change, and biodiversity collapse, to the last minute. It will be disproportionately expensive to solve the later we leave it. Indeed, it may be too late. The challenge we face is dealing with the acres of misinformation (actually, climate lies) written by sceptics and 'alt-news' sources every day. The populists, alt-newsers and conspiracy theorists just want to plant seeds of doubt rather than disprove anything. This is a cultural battle. It really matters. Sowing doubt and division is a platform for chaos. Right now it's a war on sustainability and 'wokeness', but it won't stop there. What has this got to do with business? The post-truth agenda creates instability and policy indecision. Business needs certainty not chaos. The current shift to the Right, towards post-truth, isn't just a risk to political stability, it is also a risk to business stability and business hates instability – it is the enemy of planning.

Business cannot afford to plan with short-term horizons in mind. The coming environmental challenges threaten to de-rail or break numerous business models. A case study here is fast fashion. While access to cheap clothing has a social and financial benefit for those buying them, the same can't be said for those making them (although there is a big 'watch out' here as many of the more premium and even high-end fashion houses use the same factories, the same labour and pay the same manufacturing labour costs as the fast fashion houses). And clearly there are significant environmental implications of cheap clothes as we tend to keep them for a shorter period and maybe never even wear them. This means that we buy more. According to UNEP we buy 60 per cent more clothing per person than we did 15 years ago, and keep things for half as long as we used to. It is no surprise, therefore, that the fast fashion houses are panicking. They are introducing re-worn and vintage lines. This is good. However, the words of H&M's CEO Karl-Johan Persson are telling. He said in a 2019 interview that more sustainable consumer behaviour will have 'terrible social consequences'.[2] He went on to link fast fashion to the eradication of poverty. Tell that to the people paid buttons to make the world's clothes. This argument rests on the theory that people on lower incomes can afford more and 'trendier' clothes and that in turn they will feel better about themselves as a result of looking good. This is incredibly hard to demonstrate and the Bergen Project – an organization that exists to fight global poverty – argues that the majority of people shopping in fast fashion houses could afford to pay for products made with fair trade labour and principles.

Business-as-usual is about to be disrupted by climate change, biodiversity challenges and pollution. As I say, it will be cheaper and less disruptive to tackle sooner rather than later. The problem is that it thrusts businesses into the unknown earlier and business is more disposed to kick the difficult unknowns into the long grass. Yet business should have the speed, brains and innovation to turn on a dime. Instead it waits until someone else solves the problem and then, like lemmings, they will all rush into the same space and deliver the same solution.

Why is this? It's due to a fundamental shift in the way that businesses are run. Rather than being brave and standing on principles, they have become risk averse and have, in a large part, become run by Teflon-shouldered managers who don't want to break or change anything, while at the same time talking business lingo-bingo about being purpose-led and disruptive. By leading in this way they also avoid succeeding at all. To quote Hunter S Thompson, 'Life should not be a journey to the grave with the intention of arriving safely in a pretty and well preserved body, but rather to skid in broadside in a cloud of smoke, thoroughly used up, totally worn out, and loudly proclaiming "Wow! What a Ride!"'

So, what is the solution? Going back to the start of the chapter, what is missing is bravery. Creative bravery, business bravery, bravery in leadership. All have been eroded, driven by a number of economic, social and political changes that have made the business environment more uncertain and unpredictable. This is for a number of reasons: increased regulatory scrutiny; heightened competition; economic uncertainty; reputation risk; legal risk.

Collectively, these factors have led to a more risk-averse approach among businesses. While risk-taking is still an important part of business growth and innovation, businesses are now more focused on managing and minimizing risk, rather than pursuing high-risk/high-reward strategies. This cautious approach may limit the potential for growth and expansion, but it also helps businesses to protect their assets and maintain stability in an uncertain environment.

Crisis presents opportunity and creativity is the way to exploit that opportunity

The late US President John F Kennedy famously noted that the Chinese word for 'crisis' (Weiji) is made up of two characters, one of which stands for risk and the other for opportunity. His understanding was definitely incorrect, but the attitude is still valid: a crisis presents a decision. And we do have a decision to make.

As we saw in the first part of this book nearly every one of the Earth's early-warning systems are screaming 'Help!' Therefore we can't continue making, consuming and disposing things in the same way. This alone is a significant systematic shock that should be enough to shift business thinking, but it hasn't been. Twinned with this is an increase in cost and decrease in availability of many raw materials. Again this should have been enough to kick business in the pants and realign it with different models of consumption. It hasn't been. Maybe the final change, the desires of consumers for less-damaging products and services, will. This is a complex one as this desire is as much about feeling less guilty about excessive or 'bad' consumption as it is about embracing good or less. It is often, as we have seen, about totemic action rather than tackling issues systemically with real science. The consumer is mis-educated and this is not their fault. Environmental experts have failed to communicate the scale, complexity and urgency of the problems we face; most of the media want everything in simple sound bites and this further dumbs-down the message. So I'll make it really clear:

Human activity on the planet has impacted every natural system that keeps us cool, that supports biodiversity, that ensures the replenishment of natural resources. We are in crisis. But we have the skills and the ability to avert the worst of this danger. JFK definitely misinterpreted the Chinese characters for crisis. In reality the Chinese word Weiji should be interpreted as 'danger change-point'. That is absolutely where we are. At a significant danger change-point. How many more messages and signals do we need to receive before we act?

Change points, intersections and crises offer the greatest opportunity for creativity to flourish. Remember, I'm not talking about artists and designers, I'm talking about imagining and fashioning a better world and using business to achieve that. This is creativity.

I've covered the way to start this journey and in the accompanying website (www.markshayler.com/deadplanet) we hear from a number of leaders regarding the way they see business and the way business needs to change. But I want to return to the notion or concept of the regenerative business.

CHAPTER TEN

The regenerative business

Every business that I'm working with is re-imagining what they are, are innovating around the idea of a regenerative business. This gives the greatest opportunity for creativity and growth.

The principles of regenerative business are based on the creation of sustainable systems that not only minimize harm but actively contribute to the regeneration of ecosystems and communities. As we face the challenges of climate change, resource depletion and social inequality, regenerative business practices are becoming increasingly important and seen as the antidote to the practices that have created these challenges.

Regenerative business can take many forms, from reducing impact and doing less bad (using renewable energy and reducing waste) to developing products and services that benefit the environment and society's health. Regenerative business is fundamentally about creating systems that have a positive impact on the world around us. No-one (I hope) would start a business that did harm, that failed to lift people, that left the world in a worse place than it found it – would they? Of course they would, but there are fewer of them now. There is a shift towards purpose-driven entrepreneurship. This is to be welcomed. There is also a growing interest in (if not understanding of) regenerative business.

One of the primary advantages of regenerative business is the ability to build more resilient systems. We can reduce the risks of environmental and social crises by developing businesses that support the health and well-being of ecosystems and communities. A regenerative agricultural system, for example, that promotes biodiversity and soil health is likely to be more resilient to climate change than one that relies on monoculture and chemical inputs.

Regenerative business can also generate economic opportunities by opening up new markets for environmentally friendly goods and services.

Regenerative business can provide social benefits in addition to economic benefits. Regenerative businesses can create jobs, support local economies and improve people's and the planet's health and well-being by prioritizing the needs of communities and ecosystems. A regenerative tourism business, for example, that supports natural area conservation and engages with local communities can create economic opportunities while also preserving cultural heritage and supporting ecosystem health. But it also has a mandate to educate, to create the conditions required for sustainable businesses to grow and to profit without damaging the area. We should all be operating our businesses as if we were in an ecologically sensitive area. I write this sat in an ecologically sensitive area of Thailand. It's an island called Ko Adang and it is heavily protected. Yet, despite every visitor being made aware of this, despite them having to pay a specific fee to fund protection, there is some poor behaviour in terms of littering. They are quite literally sat in the middle of a nature reserve while littering the beach before heading back to their accommodation on another island. What has this got to do with business? Business needs to bring its customers with it. Business can't solve these problems alone and if customers can't behave here what are the chances of them behaving at home?

In terms of regenerative business there is also a need for education and public awareness. Many people are unfamiliar with the concept of regenerative business and may be unaware of the advantages it can provide. We must invest in education and awareness campaigns that help people understand the importance of regenerative business and encourage them to support businesses that are committed to sustainability. It is significantly more important than shopping locally, although the two combined would be amazing.

The transition to regenerative business will be fraught with difficulties. The current economic system, which prioritizes short-term profits over long-term sustainability, is one of the most significant impediments. We need significant systemic change. To build regenerative businesses, we must develop new economic models that prioritize sustainability and social impact. This will necessitate changes in policy, regulations and financial systems.

Furthermore, collaboration and partnership are required. Building regenerative businesses necessitates collaboration among stakeholders such as businesses, governments, communities and NGOs. We need to create spaces for dialogue and collaboration that bring these disparate groups together to work towards common goals.

The UK-based think-tank Forum for the Future has looked at the journey that businesses need to take to move to a regenerative business model. They talk about four phases. They call this the Business Transformation Compass (see Figure 10.1).

Although I see this less as a ladder or straight line. In my experience business will sit across a number of these steps at the same time (see Figure 10.2).

FIGURE 10.1   Business Transformation Compass

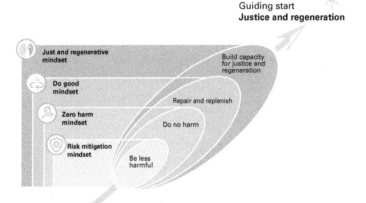

Source: Forum for the Future. A compass for just and regenerative business – report, 2021. www.forumforthefuture.org/a-compass-for-just-and-regenerative-business-report

FIGURE 10.2 From less harm to more good

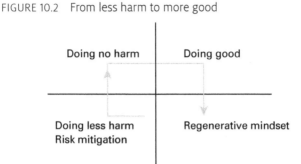

The aim is to grow the area above the bottom right while shrinking the areas above the other quadrants.

The Forum for the Future model dives into far greater detail and splits regenerative business down into seven key areas:

1 Climate
2 Nature
3 Circularity and waste
4 Land and natural resource management
5 Providing and promoting decent work
6 Voices, governance and participation
7 Human rights

For each of these Forum for the Future provides a series of prompts and hints to help you move forwards. Forum and one of its founders, Jonathon Porritt, lead in this arena; search for and download their report *Guide to Critical Shifts*. It is excellent work and goes on to break the required actions down into discrete business functions.

It is a helpful explanation of trajectory and essentially mirrors the description of the questions asked of me by clients over the last 30 years. From helping me manage risks, to helping me do no harm, to helping me do good and finally to creating a just and regenerative mindset. I really like the description of this last phase and it widens the concept of regenerative business from environmental justice to social justice. Let's look at these in a little more detail.

Environmental justice

This sits at the heart of making sustainable profits. Creating fairness and justice between generations and within populations is central to building a sustainable business.

Environmental justice is the fair and equitable distribution of environmental benefits and burdens among all individuals, communities and generations regardless of their race, ethnicity, socioeconomic status or any other demographic factor.

The concept recognizes that some communities, particularly those belonging to marginalized groups, face disproportionate exposure to environmental hazards, while others enjoy the benefits of environmental amenities such as clean air and water.

Environmental justice emerged in the United States in the 1980s, primarily in response to the unequal distribution of toxic waste sites and other environmental hazards in low-income communities and communities of colour. The movement has since expanded globally and encompasses a broader range of environmental issues, including climate change, biodiversity loss and resource depletion.

At its core, environmental justice seeks to rectify environmental inequalities by empowering affected communities to participate in decision-making processes that affect their health and well-being. This includes giving communities a voice in environmental policy development and implementation, as well as access to environmental information and resources that can help them protect their rights and interests. Environmental justice also recognizes the need for systemic change in how we approach environmental issues. It calls for a more holistic and inclusive approach to environmental protection, one that acknowledges the interconnectedness of social, economic and environmental systems.

Overall, environmental justice is an essential concept for building a more equitable and sustainable world. Traditionally sustainability has been split into three areas: environmental sustainability, social sustainability and economic sustainability. Add into that the aim of not compromising the ability of future generations to meet their needs. These are great principles. But over time sustainability has sadly become another word for environmental issues.

Achieving environmental justice requires a multifaceted approach that addresses the root causes of environmental inequalities and degradation. Environmental justice is essential to building a more sustainable and equitable world. It acknowledges that environmental problems are not just scientific but are social and political too.

Social justice

Social justice refers to the principle of ensuring that all individuals and groups have equitable access to rights, opportunities and resources. The concept is grounded in the idea that everyone deserves to be treated fairly and with dignity, regardless of their race, gender, ethnicity, sexual orientation, socioeconomic status, religion or other aspects of their identity. The goal of social justice is to create a more equitable and just society, where everyone has the opportunity to thrive and succeed.

Social justice includes a wide range of issues, such as ending discrimination and prejudice, promoting equal access to education, healthcare and employment opportunities, addressing poverty and economic inequality, protecting the rights of marginalized groups and advocating for social change.

At its core, social justice is about fairness and equality. It recognizes that certain groups have historically faced significant barriers to success and equal opportunity and aims to address these disparities through policies and programmes that promote equity and inclusion. This can involve initiatives like affirmative action, which seeks to level the playing field for historically marginalized groups, or efforts to address systemic racism and discrimination in areas like access to resources, environmental damage, employment, housing, criminal justice and healthcare.

Economic justice

Economic justice seeks to ensure that every individual has equal opportunities to access economic resources, benefits and opportunities, regardless of their social status, gender, race or other distinguishing characteristics, enabling everyone to live a dignified life.

The key principles of economic justice include equity, equality and fairness. Equity refers to the idea that individuals should be rewarded based on their effort, skill and contributions to society, rather than their social status or privilege. Equality, on the other hand, seeks to ensure that everyone has equal access to resources, opportunities and benefits, regardless of their background or circumstances. Fairness, in turn, involves ensuring that the rules and regulations governing the economy are just and impartial, and that individuals are treated fairly and equally under the law.

In terms of business, this cuts straight to the heart of governance and the way a business attracts talent to enable it to grow and thrive.

Another approach is to ensure that the economic system provides equal access to education, training and job opportunities for all individuals, regardless of their social status or background. This can be achieved through policies such as affirmative action, education subsidies and job training programmes.

Finally, economic justice can also be promoted by ensuring that the economic system is environmentally sustainable and does not cause harm to future generations. This can be achieved through policies such as environmental regulations, carbon pricing and investment in renewable energy. It's this last element that overlaps most with sustainability.

Regenerative Business Navigator

Building on the work of Forum I've developed this simple Navigator and canvas to help structure your transition from a business that has an environmental policy, strategy and processes (you will have developed these earlier in the book) to one striving to become a regenerative business.

The Navigator matrix below summarizes actions that can be taken against different functions of the business and change themes.

- Strategy:
  - **Climate change:** Set net zero and net positive targets that are ambitious, based on reduction then nature-based solutions.
  - **Biodiversity:** Understand your biodiversity impact and establish clear net gain initiatives and effective projects.
  - **Circularity:** Waste strategy should be closed-loop (zero waste to landfill).
  - **Resource use:** If you can't get stuff you can't make things, if you can't make things you can't make a difference. Build a strategy on efficient resource use.
  - **Supply chain:** Develop resilient and kind supply chains.

- **Work for good:** Employment brings more than money. It brings self-respect, growth, safety and it builds your company. Develop an employment strategy built on trust and respect. Reward in more ways than money.

- **Governance:** The importance of developing a strategy around open, clear and diverse governance has never been more important. This embraces taxation, participation, supply chain and diversity.

- **Ethics:** The way we do business with others, the way we pay suppliers and treat our team, the way we harvest/extract our raw materials needs to be ethical.

- Leadership:

  - **Climate change:** Ensure the team have opportunity to shape this. Explain why this matters to business and put systems in place to harness the team's ideas.

  - **Biodiversity:** Nature can sometimes feel at odds with business. Leadership's role here is to explain why nature matters to business.

  - **Circularity:** Build a culture where waste is seen as a design flaw or a systems flaw. Incentivize ideas and behaviour.

  - **Resource use:** This isn't just about using less, it is also about using better and more responsibly.

  - **Supply chain:** Talk about the power of supply chains and value chains, indicating that the business is built on top of, and because of, great suppliers.

  - **Work for good:** You need to demonstrate trust and respect, you need to develop a culture as far from 'us and them' as you can, you need solid mental health and support policies in place.

- ○ **Governance:** Model this, display this. Leadership needs to be open, diverse, participatory and honest.

- ○ **Ethics:** This strategy needs to be modelled. Ethical businesses are consistently found to out-perform others. Purpose and ethics need to be owned by the whole business.

• Business models:

- ○ **Climate change:** You can't make money from a dead planet and climate change is the fastest way to kill the planet for us. Your business model needs to be net-zero at worst. How can you make more (or the same) money with less carbon impact?

- ○ **Biodiversity:** Once you've understood your biodiversity impacts you can modify your business models to initially reduce impact but ultimately enhance biodiversity.

- ○ **Circularity:** Circular systems (for the things you sell) require whole new business models. There is more profit to be made here if you're smart.

- ○ **Resource use:** Building business models that protect resources or shift focus to renewable or less damaging resources really matters. There may be cost increases of supplies and hence business model refinement may be required.

- ○ **Supply chain:** Raw materials are becoming scarce and expensive to extract. The way you manage and support your supply chain has a direct impact upon costs but also business continuity. This is business critical and hence is central to your business model.

- **Work for good:** Work brings more than money, but it does bring money. Build a business case for considerate employment and a broad package of reward.

- **Governance:** Bad governance costs a business money. Cheap or no governance is the most expensive governance. Get this right early and save money.

- **Ethics:** Some improvements in ethics come with higher costs. This needs building into the business model but will ultimately reduce costs in the long term.

- Innovation:

- **Climate change:** Placing sustainability at the heart of the innovation process is essential. Placing carbon reduction and ultimately net zero at the heart of the innovation process is urgent.

- **Biodiversity:** Constraints are good and ultimately spark innovation. Adding net gain as an innovation hard-line sparks innovation.

- **Circularity:** Innovation here is essential in terms of raw materials, design, manufacturing, use-phase, end of life and (probably most importantly) business models. Your innovation strategy needs to be explicit about this.

- **Resource use:** Innovation in terms of new raw materials, innovative processing, closed-loop manufacture and links back to circularity.

- o **Supply chain:** Supply chain innovation in terms of better and less damaging raw materials.

- o **Work for good:** Innovation in terms of purpose, the way people are valued, working practices.

- o **Governance:** Governance is the overlooked element of ESG and needs revolutionizing. There are many new governance models but they tend to only be adopted by community interest companies, cooperatives or employee-owned businesses. There is much strength here if these can be introduced to other business structures.

- o **Ethics:** Ethical business requires innovation in terms of working practices and procedures.

- Design:

  - o **Climate change:** Designing harm out of the product or service is the key to reducing impact costs effectively. Reduce carbon intensity of raw materials, subassemblies, products, products-use, service design and end of life.

  - o **Biodiversity:** Apply biophyllic design principles to both minimize impact upon nature and enhance biodiversity.

  - o **Circularity:** Design is the key to circularity: product design, service design, design for refurbishment and repair, design for end of life. (There is nothing more expensive than cheap design.)

  - o **Resource use:** Designing bad resources out of and less damaging resources into a product or service.

- **Supply chain:** Design thinking is a great tool to apply to business practices including supply chain. Spend time in the design and planning phase of supply chain formation and planning.

- **Work for good:** This is about designing a business with purpose and a culture that values the team.

- **Governance:** How you design and shape the governance structures determines their effectiveness. Can you use design to create greater participation and diversity?

- **Ethics:** Again, this goes back to business and culture design. Culture doesn't just emerge, it is a combination of purpose, people and leadership. All of which can have design thinking applied to them.

- Operations:

  - **Climate change:** Your operations have a carbon and energy impact. Better practices and processes reduce this. See above on process design.

  - **Biodiversity:** Consider how your direct operations impact the environment. This can happen through various activities such as habitat destruction, pollution and the use of natural resources.

  - **Circularity:** Can you build products in such a way as to make them simpler and easier to disassemble, repair, remanufacture and recycle? Is the machinery and IT you designed for circularity? Can you return it to the maker/seller at its end of life?

- **Resource use:** How can you apply lean manufacturing and operations to your business to reduce resource use? How can you go beyond this and use renewable or closed-loop resources? Can you stimulate replenishment?

- **Supply chain:** Supply chains feed the business. Any disruption can cripple the business. Therefore, understanding supply chain security and moving away from supply chains that may be impacted by extreme environmental events and that are either environmentally or socially disruptive are key.

- **Work for good:** How can the core of what you do and how you do it be enhanced to help people feel better about themselves and help their mental health? How can we broaden engagement and enhance diversity? What's your plan?

- **Governance:** Governing a business needs to be done openly and with engagement from the team. Effective governance requires broad representation and collective agreement. How can you involve operations in governance? Remember, without operations you have no business. It's easy to think that marketing is the most important team in the business. This is not the case.

- **Ethics:** Ethics needs to run through your business from left to right and front to back. Operations is no different. Where are the ethical 'watch outs' within the business? Sales? Marketing? Supply chain? Draw an ethical heat-map of the business. Where are the weaknesses and where are the strengths?

- Communications/marketing:
  - **Climate change:** This is a risk area. Once a business begins this transition marketing and communications want to talk publicly about these things quickly. Be very careful here. Say nothing for a year. How can you communicate what you are doing with authority, with humility and science?
  - **Biodiversity:** Once more, don't over-claim any gains here, and understand the impact that this function has upon biodiversity.
  - **Circularity:** Can you build circularity into contracts for any equipment the comms/marketing team use? Can you gift old equipment and maybe tell this story (always put yourself last in these stories, focus on the difference the gifting makes). Can you tell stories about how your product/service is part of the circular economy, how is it making the world better?
  - **Resource use:** Again, be modest about any gains here. What are you doing? Why? What will the benefits be in terms of resource scarcity, resource availability? What can others learn from the things you've done? Share, don't boast.
  - **Supply chain:** Tell stories about the benefits of supply chain sustainability: from provenance and reduced impact to security of supply and fair trade pay.
  - **Work for good:** How can comms improve how it works to build a culture based on purpose, to attract diverse minds?

- Governance: Great governance requires brilliant internal and external communications. This communication needs to be two-way and needs the comms team to be on 'receive' as well as on 'send'.

- Ethics: Explain your ethics really clearly. Make it a point of pride but not one of boasting. It's just how you do business. Nothing more.

- HR:

  - Climate change: Build a responsibility for shared action on climate change into all contracts, into bonus systems, into culture. Embed climate responsibility into all job descriptions.

  - Biodiversity: Build an awareness of and shared responsibility for biodiversity, via the company handbook and onboarding process and into all contracts.

  - Circularity: Work with procurement to equip the team with circular or long-life equipment. Embed circular skills/awareness into all job descriptions.

  - Resource use: Build a responsibility for shared action on resource efficiency into all contracts, into bonus systems, into culture.

  - Supply chain: When recruiting staff who will have a supply chain or procurement role ensure they are as focused on responsible supply chains as they are 'cheap' supply chains.

  - Work for good: HR are the central point for ensuring that work lifts people. They shouldn't just focus on recruitment but also on talent retention. People leave because of bad culture.

- ○ **Governance:** HR have a significant responsibility to oversee and lead conversations around governance and transparency. This is an enabling rather than policing role.

- ○ **Ethics:** HR also have an enabling role regarding the ethical 'fit' of the talent as it enters the team. Furthermore there is a need to maintain this and ensure it doesn't change.

- Finance:

  - ○ **Climate change:** The big change here is to elongate payback thresholds from where they are (probably around two years) to 5 to 10 years minimum. Capital investments, for example, in carbon reduction pay back more slowly than other capital investments but pay back for longer.

  - ○ **Biodiversity:** Again there is a need to change expectations regarding payback, think longer term. How can you enable more and better action by changing the way finance decisions are made?

  - ○ **Circularity:** Again, elongate payback thresholds. Circular economy improvements of your product change the business model; circular economy contracts of kit shift expenditure from capital to revenue.

  - ○ **Resource use:** Reducing resource use and ensuring resource availability reduce costs and financial risks.

  - ○ **Supply chain:** Effective management of supply chains reduces financial exposure and ensures greater financial transparency. The finance team can unlock significant progress here.

- ○ **Work for good:** A happy team stays – it costs more to attract than retain talent.

- ○ **Governance:** The financial director is central to the leadership team and therefore has a responsibility to ensure governance structures are responsible and grow the business in a regenerative way.

- ○ **Ethics:** Ethical businesses, businesses with a purpose, businesses that invest in sustainability are the most profitable. How can the financial director enable work in this area?

The functions and how they relate to sustainability are covered in greater detail here:

Strategy

The strategy function of the business sets the way that it will fulfil its purpose and bring its vision to life. I know what you're thinking: 'What if we don't have a vision and strategy?' Well, turn back to Chapter 7 and I take you through these. But strategy really matters. Yes, I know, according to Peter Drucker, 'culture eats strategy for breakfast', but you need both. So you are well advised to have a clear strategic vision wrapped around a purpose that is bigger than money. Developing clear strategies and recruiting the very best people to help deliver them are essential to all elements of your business and transitioning to a regenerative business is no different. Please remember that sustainability needs to sit at the heart of the business. You aren't a business with a sustainability strategy, you're a sustainable business with a strategy. We aren't bolting sustainability on to your business. You are becoming a sustainable business.

Leadership

When you think about those businesses that lead the sustainability debate what do you see? Passion, bravery and leadership. The bravest businesses, the most admirable, have the strongest leadership. This doesn't need to be a single leader (although it sometimes is), it's as much about a clear and driven leadership group.

We have too many managers and not enough leaders. Leadership means inspiring, influencing and guiding a group of people towards a shared goal. A leader is someone who has the vision, knowledge and skills to motivate their team to achieve their objectives.

Effective leadership is not limited to any particular style or approach. Rather, it is a combination of various traits and qualities including empathy, integrity, communication, creativity and problem solving. A good leader can garner great vision and ideas from their team.

Ultimately, leadership is about creating a positive and productive environment where everyone feels valued, supported and motivated to achieve their best. Placing that in the context of developing a regenerative business these changes are not going to be easy and this means we need the best leaders aligning with the bravest strategy.

Business models

The way we make money matters. But more than that, making money matters. Profit is good. Or it can be. It depends what we spend it on and, of course, on how we make it. But returning to a through-line of this book, enterprise can make things better or worse; it's up to us. Therefore developing business models that align with a strategy that supports a purpose that has regeneration at its heart is essential. This is not necessarily constraining – although constraint is indeed a great way of enhancing and accelerating innovation, or at the very least helping to focus it.

There are many ways to develop business models and I have already shown you the Business Canvas that I use to start this process. The key thing is to think through the stages and give equal attention to them. The vision and the finances both matter, the customer segmentation and competitor analysis both matter. Try not to fall into the trap of thinking that you're 'not a numbers person'. You are, or you need to become one, and fast.

Business modelling is a creative process, view it in the same way that you'd view a design project – because it is. Place sustainability, social progression and ethics at the heart of the process: almost like a mantra that you repeat at each stage, 'how does this help' kind of thing.

Innovation

This is the lifeblood of business and yet we've become lazy at it. Fall in love with innovation for good. How can ideas inspire and lead change? How can innovation make things better? I don't know which innovation process you use (The Design Council 'Double Diamond' is a great place to start) but begin with a great question or problem. Make sure you are answering a real need. Innovation isn't a new flavour of ice cream, a new cut of a pair of jeans, a new shape of mug. These are design improvements and are great, but we need true innovation. Actually, we need disruptive innovation to shift thinking.

Let's look at denim jeans here as an example. There are many artisan jeans makers and they're all great. Some are more modest than others. Some charge more for the same jeans. Some speak in grandiose terms about their sustainability approach. But only one is attempting real disruptive innovation. Mud Jeans in the Netherlands lease their jeans to the customer. This means that more people can afford them, and it means that the company can have an ongoing relationship with the consumer that doesn't end with the sale. It also means that the financing of the business changes. The company have the same upfront expenses but recover their money more slowly. There is a significant need for innovation in business models and that requires a financial director who is brave and innovative. That's a rare combination of skills in that role but not unheard of.

Design

I have made this point before but it bears repeating: design is the single most powerful sustainability tool there is. Much has been said about the notion of design thinking and it is a little overhyped, but this approach to problem solving is incredibly constructive. What is it?

Design thinking is a problem-solving approach that emphasizes empathy, creativity and iterative prototyping to address complex challenges like sustainability. The process usually includes five stages: empathize, define, ideate, prototype and test. The empathize stage involves understanding the needs, emotions and experiences of the people or systems for whom the design is intended. To do this you need to observe, listen, engage and gain insights into problems and motivations. In the define stage, the insights gained from the empathize stage are synthesized to define in greater depth the problem to be solved or the opportunity to exploit. The ideate stage means generating ideas and solutions to address the problem. This stage emphasizes divergent thinking, where a large number of ideas are generated without judgment or criticism. The prototype stage involves creating tangible representations of the ideas generated in the ideate stage. This can include sketches, models or even digital simulations.

The final stage, test, involves testing the prototypes with the people for whom the design is intended. Feedback from the testing stage is used to refine the design and inform future iterations. Remember, there is nothing more expensive than cheap design.

Operations

Operations are the heart of any business. The core functions that make the business work, that develop and deliver products or services, that support customers, that procure and plan; these are the most important elements of the business. We forget this. It is easy to focus on and elevate, for example, marketing. This is akin to celebrating the people that polish shoes and design the window display rather than the shoemaker.

The roles in the various elements of operations have the ability to significantly enhance the company's environmental performance. The way that I look at operations from a sustainability perspective varies depending upon the nature of the business. With a design-led business operations have significant environmental power as they are taking customer briefs and developing designs that can significantly reduce environmental impact. Therefore building sustainability considerations into the work process is where I would go here. For a company selling, for example, mobile phones, operations will stretch from procurement to sales and distribution. Understanding the environmental impact of each of the operational functions is a start but the really interesting approach is to look at the potential good that can be done by each function.

In short, take a look at the operations of your business. List the environmental impacts and try and reduce those. Then look at the opportunities that each function has control over. How can each function do more good as well as less bad.

Communications and marketing

Rather than spending time and effort on selling things we don't need to people who don't really want them and can't afford them, on a planet that is struggling, what if we had spent this time and effort communicating the challenges that we face and how to solve them. Quite simply, we wouldn't be in this mess.

My message for marketing is really clear: stop lying.

Marketing and communications have a responsibility to tell the truth, to explain complexity, and muster collective action, and to make clear that we can't just simply buy and consume our way out of this problem. It isn't good enough to say it; you actually need to do something, report on it and own it. Never letting the truth get in the way of a good story is why we have messed up so many times. And yet I still see brand marketing making inane statements around sustainability. This nonsense must end and marketing as a profession needs to have a good long hard look at itself and its behaviour. Yes, I know I sound like a schoolteacher but I'm okay with that.

Human resources

Talent acquisition and retention is central to business success and to our ability to tackle problems swiftly, with empathy, with creativity and tackle them well. Sustainability is one of these problems. HR gets a ringside seat in the way that a business is run, the trajectory that it is taking and the future needs it has. Every contract and all job descriptions need to be explicit in having an environmental and sustainability responsibility. HR can drive this internally. If the business isn't fit for the future, if it doesn't reduce impact and risk, then it won't be hiring anyone.

HR is the key to bringing talent in that matches the company's aspirations. But some HR practitioners need to move beyond their own limiting beliefs. HR has steadily become a defensive function rather than an enabling one. It should predominantly move away from removing problems when they arise to creating conditions where problems don't arise, and rather than playing safe, bring in exhilarating talent.

Finance

I'm going to talk about the finance function a bit more at length than I've done for the other functions. Why is this? Quite simply that the way we spend our money as a business is instrumental in both reducing our impact and the way we measure payback or return on investment. Forecasted future trajectories will either accelerate or impede the transition to becoming a regenerative business. The inflexibility of financial mechanisms to back long-term thinking is a massive part of what got us into this mess. Short-termism is the enemy of stability, be that ecological or economic. It exacerbates boom–bust cycles and it ensures the rapid conversion of value from resources, from slowly grown value embedded in the natural world, to financial value distributed to the few.

There is a revolution required in the way that we measure and distribute value. I covered this in Chapter 2 but it is worth returning to here. From the perspective of yield and return there are clear arguments for shifting the focal point of corporate finance from traditional investments to climate- and sustainability-focused investments. For example, Forbes reported that in 2022 many sustainable investments outperformed comparable investments without a sustainability focus. But the problem with the 'market' is that it will continue to speculate upon futures even as the ship sinks. It lacks any understanding of the long term, it lacks a moral compass and the moral compass of those self-acclaimed Masters of the Universe has been demagnetized, it seems. Part of the problem is the system itself, but another part is the operators within the system.

So, what do we do? We need to recalibrate the role of finance. Money only does good when it is moving, when it supports things that support society and the planet. Profit is not a dirty word, profit should drive growth and spread 'goodness' throughout society. Finance is as amazing as it can do so much good, if directed to do so.

As a business we can't change the macro system but we can become better examples of a form of capitalism that values people and planet alongside profit. To do so would need a change to the way finance works inside businesses.

Financial directors can play a crucial role in the fight for a more sustainable world by incorporating sustainability into their organization's financial strategies and decision-making processes. Here are a few ways they can do this:

1 *Adopting a 'green finance' approach:* Financial directors can prioritize investments in low-carbon projects and technologies and allocate capital towards sustainable and environmentally regenerative solutions. This can include supporting the development of renewable energy, energy efficiency and circular economy initiatives.

2 *Setting sustainability goals:* By setting ambitious sustainability goals, financial directors can encourage their organization to prioritize environmental concerns in their operations. This can include reducing carbon emissions, increasing resource efficiency, engaging customers on sustainability issues, adopting product to service business models, supporting net gain initiatives, reducing consumption/raw materials used per unit of turnover and improving waste management practices.

3 *Disclosing sustainability information:* Financial directors can also promote transparency and accountability by disclosing sustainability-related information to stakeholders, such as investors, customers and regulators. This can include reporting on environmental impact, sustainability performance and climate-related risks and opportunities. The advent of carbon as a universally

adopted metric for environmental impact is partially due to the fact that it can be counted. The problem is that counted and accounted for should be the same thing, yet there is a significant lack of accountability for previous carbon emissions and for offshore, supply-chain or shadow carbon impact.

4 *Collaborating with stakeholders:* Financial directors must work with stakeholders to promote sustainability in their supply chains and encourage suppliers to adopt more sustainable practices. This can help reduce the environmental footprint of their organization and promote sustainable development more broadly. This could be as simple as developing supply-chain tools and training for suppliers or becoming a form of bank that could offer preferential loans and investments to the supply chain.

5 *Working with the management team to set effective business unit targets and strategies:* These would be reported upon each month or quarter in parallel with the financial reports that the business produces.

In the 1990s/2000s, environment was seen either as PR or as technical. But it is much more important than both of these. It needs to sit at the very heart of the business.

Every function of the business needs to not just embrace sustainability but take it to its centre, to wrap its business plan around it. The Navigator above will help you develop an approach to moving your business away from business as usual and towards becoming a regenerative business.

Finance is an unlikely place for sustainability to really take hold but this is probably the most important function within the business when it comes to moving from degenerative to regenerative. Sure there will be technical and talent-based challenges but it is a revolution in the way that we view money, return on investment and the allocation of these returns that must change. Please don't think that I'm pleading for a rush to the creation of not-for-profit businesses; I've said repeatedly that profit isn't bad. It is the way it is distributed and the short-termism surrounding its creation that I have problems with. Indeed, the need to build social and environmental justice into capitalism is urgent, and the only way that it will survive.

Making money isn't the issue, it's how we make money that matters

The challenges we face require a new approach to making money. It's not making money that's the problem, it's the way we make money. The market, the mechanism of wealth creation and distribution, needs refinement. I'm a massive fan of the benefits well-guided entrepreneurship can bring, but I'm also aware that the private sector doesn't have the monopoly on entrepreneurship.

The public sector can unlock new entrepreneurship. The notion that the private sector serves as the only or primary engine of innovation was debunked in 2013 with the release of Mariana Mazzucato's book *The Entrepreneurial State*. She makes the case that public sector investments in fundamental research and subsequent technological development prior to commercialization by the private sector played a significant role in the United States' post-Second World War economic success. The same is true of many European states and of course Japan and China. Government funding helped lay the technological foundations that were beyond business's means or interests in major industries (manufacturing, information technology, pharmaceuticals and telecommunications) without diminishing the entrepreneurial, manufacturing and marketing skills of private businesses. Similar unlocking and enabling public investments are still being made today in the development of smart technology, new battery designs for electric vehicles and, during the Covid-19 pandemic, the search for a vaccine. Given this shared need and interest, the time is right to rekindle public discussion about the value of public–private sector collaboration, explain these benefits to workers and citizens, and create the necessary accountability and transparency commitments to ensure that government funding does not simply consist of tax-free transfer payments or subsidies to private companies. A new approach to the partnership, the symbiotic relationship, between the public and private sectors is long overdue.

There are, of course, a number of ways that capitalism can be made to work a little harder for the planet.

One way to make capitalism more sustainable is to incorporate sustainability into business practices. This book creates a guide to doing just that, and the use of sustainable materials, reducing waste and emissions, and investing in renewable energy makes both economic and environmental sense. Businesses can also adopt a circular economy model which should have its emphasis on the economy word as much as the circular word.

Another way to promote sustainability in capitalism is to create financial incentives for businesses to adopt sustainable practices. Governments can offer tax breaks, subsidies and other financial incentives for companies that invest in renewable energy, reduce their carbon footprint and adopt sustainable business practices. Investors can also consider sustainable investing, which involves investing in companies that prioritize environmental, social and governance factors.

Collaboration and innovation are key to making capitalism more sustainable. Governments, businesses and individuals can work together to develop new technologies, products and services that are environmentally friendly and promote sustainability. This can include the development of clean energy technologies, sustainable transportation and eco-friendly products. Since the 2016 Brexit vote, UK business has been isolated from many funds and projects that stimulate innovation. However, the UK innovation programme Innovate UK is showing great foresight and focusing a significant number of their competitions on sustainability-related issues. Indeed, sustainability is a component of the assessment of all their competitions.

Finally, regulation can be used to ensure that businesses adopt sustainable practices. Governments can impose regulations on the production and disposal of waste, on emissions and on other environmental pollutants. While this can help it is truly a last resort.

Summary of the Navigator

I'm a fan of straight talking. I have an absolute hatred of business language. The use of pointless and often meaningless terms (going forward, robust response, mission critical, boil the ocean, sticking to our knitting, leverage) to confuse and fill space irritates me. Say what you mean, mean what you say. So I'll do just that. Every job is now a sustainability job, climate change is everyone's business. The transition to regenerative business is urgent and all consuming. It will also ensure that business survives as well as the planet surviving. With that urgency in mind, you can see my simple summary of the shifts needed by function in Table 10.1.

This shift requires an entirely different mindset throughout business. Thinking more cooperatively than competitively, or at least a blend of the two; cooperating on some issues within a broader competitive landscape; seeing resources as shared assets to protect and elongate rather than squander; seeing talent as something that is precious and requires nurturing rather than mistreating; and seeing value in things other than money.

We require significant changes in behaviour, but it is essential to remember that our behaviour is part of a series of interconnected systems. Systems change has a huge role to play in stimulating consumption and exacerbating environmental damage. The Covid lockdowns revealed that behaviour change alone isn't enough. Across the globe, as people stopped working and spent more time outside, there was hope that global emissions would drop considerably. While we perhaps became more aware of nature and hopefully more appreciative, global emissions only dropped

TABLE 10.1   Regenerative Business Navigator role transitions

Business function	From	To
Strategy	Short-term profit maximization. Lots of words. Putting the competition out of business.	Long-term protection of interests. Lots of action. Outlasting the competition but maybe working with them.
Leadership	Do what I say. I'll build a business that grows money and does less harm.	Come with me. Let's build a business that grows us all and does good for the planet.
Business models	Profit at all costs. We maximize profit over everything and we do it fast.	Longer-term profit strategies that don't break our people or our ability to make future profits.
Innovation	Bolting sustainability onto innovation as an afterthought or sales tool.	Building sustainability into all innovation briefs. If the new idea is worse than the old one environmentally it doesn't happen; if it isn't regenerative then it is re-worked until it is.
Design	Eco-design when applied looks at minimizing impact alone.	Regenerative design applied to all products and services.

(continued)

TABLE 10.1 (Continued)

Business function	From	To
Operations	Applying lean principles where payback is under two years.	Applying lean and green to ensure the processes are regenerative. Elongate payback periods, ensure net gain.
Communications and marketing	Communications: Telling not explaining. Marketing: Don't let the truth get in the way of a good story.	Communications: Explaining clearly and coherently the need for new models of business. Marketing: Tell stories about a better world and your role in it.
HR	Reactively filling posts. Focusing on a narrow job description.	Proactively seeking talent with a skill set and mindset that is broad and encompasses sustainability as an opportunity.
Finance	A controlling force with short time horizons.	An enabling force with longer time horizons.

by 17 per cent (although, this was an unprecedented reduction not seen since records began). This means that 83 per cent of emissions remained despite significant changes in patterns of behaviour. Much of our lives were scaled back. Putting this into context we need to reduce net-carbon emissions to zero. This requires massive system change – not just using re-usable cups and avoiding plastic.

'The last chapter'

Is this the last chapter? Not of this book, but of life as we know it. No, there are many left to come but they will be dwindling and thin affairs if we don't re-orientate our ingenuity and creativity towards solving the world's problems, and yes, making money as we do so. No-one would set fire to the house they lived in, soil their own water supply and poison all their own food.

Would they?

Well, yes. In the pursuit of profit that's exactly what has happened. Profit without any measure of social or environmental justice is not fair. Indeed, it's not profit in the fullest sense. How can it be profitable when it makes some people, communities and environments worse off? That's not profit. It is accumulation through exploitation. And yes those words sum up the history of capitalism and colonialism. But the world has changed and times have changed. Capitalism has to change too.

In my workshops and presentations I always show the slide in Figure C.1.

And this is true for the way we make money too. The companies that don't change will become increasingly disconnected from their customers and employees; will become less relevant in a rapidly changing world. But this isn't just about relevancy, it's about survival. Survival of the business, but more importantly the planet and its ability to support life, business and enterprise.

There is a need to take individual action.

There is a need to take action within the business.

There is an urgent need to think about systems change. This can feel unbelievably daunting, it can feel like someone else's problem, it can also feel futile. But it isn't. There's a tipping-point that occurs with systems changes.

FIGURE C.1   Mark's final slide

Disruption is normal now.
Change is bloody inevitable.
How it was done yesterday is not how it should be done today.
Nothings stays the same and neither should you.
The problem comes when change happens and you don't.

Systems change models

There are many systems change models, many are brilliant but I have a lot of time for the Action Scales Model developed by Nobles et al. in 2021.[1] We can apply it to sustainability.

This is a theoretical framework used to understand how people make decisions about engaging in health-promoting behaviours. However, the thinking applies to many complex problems including sustainability. The model is based on the idea that people engage in improvement (in the original analysis, health) behaviours on a continuum, from not doing anything at all to taking a significant action. The model proposes that there are five distinct stages in this continuum, and that people move through these stages in a predictable way as they become more motivated to change their behaviour. My suggestion is that sustainability and particularly the shift in the behaviour of business to move them from degenerative to regenerative, from environmentally damaging to environmental capacity building, is no different and that this model applies the same way.

The first stage in the Action Scales Model is the pre-contemplation stage. At this stage, people and businesses (let's not forget that businesses are made up of people) are not yet thinking about changing their behaviour. They may be unaware of the environmental risks associated with their current behaviour, or they may not be ready to make a change for other reasons, or they may be in denial about the risks of their behaviour.

The second stage in the model is contemplation. At this stage, people are starting to think about changing their behaviour. They may be weighing the pros and cons of making a change, and considering the challenges and benefits that come with it. This may involve an assessment of the costs and benefits.

The third stage is preparation. At this stage, the business has decided to make a change and is taking steps to prepare for it. For example, a business that has decided to go net zero may start researching different offsetting methods, and they may be assessing carbon reduction assessments and methods internally.

The fourth stage is action. At this stage, the business is actively making changes to their behaviour, their processes and their actions. This may involve a change in manufacturing process, materials, business models, service design and internal processes. I say maybe – I mean definitely.

The fifth and final stage in the model is maintenance. At this stage, businesses will have successfully made changes to their behaviour and are working to maintain it over the long term. They may be using strategies to help them stay on track, such as setting goals, tracking their progress and seeking support from their team and even other businesses.

Organizations move through these stages but may oscillate back and forth between stages before successfully reaching the maintenance stage. For example, an organization may have changed to a circular business model and have a range of service and repair options for customers, while at the same time not fully embracing or understanding the sustainability impacts of their supply chain all the way through. Being in different stages for different elements of the business is to be expected. Some transitions are simpler than others.

There are also a number of factors that the Action Scales Model proposes can exert influence as you move through these stages. For example, technical support, self-efficacy (the belief in one's ability to successfully make a change) and the perceived benefits of the behaviour change can all play a role in helping move from one stage to the next.

I have combined and built upon the Regenerative Business Navigator and Action Scales Model to produce a Regenerative Compass (see Figure C.2).

This provides a template and model that allows you to map where you are – like a spider graph. Plot where you are on it and plot where you want to be. The gap between the two is the opportunity gap. That's the focus of your innovation programme (look back a few chapters to the

FIGURE C.2   The Regenerative Compass

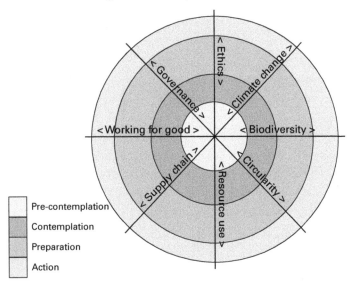

Pre-contemplation

Contemplation

Preparation

Action

double diamond process). Use this gap as motivation rather than becoming daunted by it. Closing this gap is not a sprint, it's a long-distance run. We need stamina, resolve and determination. Additionally, try and plot where your competitors are on it. Where are the blocks that the sector needs to come together to remove or minimize?

It is perfectly normal to be in different rings for each of the themes. Repeat this process annually to get an understanding of the progress you've made. Each of the themes can be broken down as per the Navigator and you can add fine detail, responsibilities, actions and strategies. See this as a 3D model with the detail hanging off the bottom of it.

Summary of actions to become a more regenerative business

The Regenerative Business Navigator and Regenerative Compass should help you plan the strategy for the changes needed in your business.

The chapters in the middle of this book give you loads of practical action to take.

To summarize the key steps you can take to reduce your impact and become a more regenerative business, here are 10 actions you can take to get you going:

1 *Adopt regenerative practices:* A regenerative business should focus on practices that restore and replenish natural resources rather than just reducing harm. These practices may include using renewable energy sources, implementing regenerative agricultural practices and reducing waste.

2 *Create a regenerative culture:* A regenerative business should foster a culture that encourages collaboration, transparency and innovation. This culture should prioritize employee well-being, customer satisfaction and environmental sustainability.

3 *Collaborate with stakeholders:* A regenerative business should actively seek out and collaborate with stakeholders, including customers, suppliers and local communities. By engaging with stakeholders, the business can better understand their needs and priorities, and develop solutions that meet their needs.

4 *Develop regenerative business models:* A regenerative business should develop a business model that is focused on creating positive social and environmental impact. This may involve developing products or services that promote sustainability or adopting a circular business model that reduces waste.

5 *Measure and report on impact:* A regenerative business should measure and report on its social and environmental impact, using metrics that go beyond traditional financial metrics. This can help the business understand the effectiveness of its regenerative practices and identify areas for improvement.

6 *Incorporate social and environmental impact into decision-making:* A regenerative business should consider the social and environmental impact of its decisions alongside financial considerations. This can help the business make more sustainable and ethical decisions.

7 *Engage in regenerative supply chain management:* A regenerative business should work with its suppliers to

develop more sustainable and regenerative supply chains. This may involve sourcing materials locally, implementing responsible sourcing practices and supporting suppliers in adopting regenerative practices.

8   *Invest in regenerative technologies:* A regenerative business should invest in technologies that support its regenerative practices, such as renewable energy, sustainable materials and regenerative agriculture techniques.

9   *Educate and engage employees:* A regenerative business should educate and engage employees about the importance of sustainability and regenerative practices. This can help create a culture of sustainability and encourage employees to contribute to the business's regenerative efforts.

10 *Collaborate with other businesses:* A regenerative business should collaborate with other businesses to drive positive social and environmental impact at scale. By working together, businesses can leverage their collective resources and expertise to create more significant change and remove sector-based problems or strategy inertia.

I wanted to end with a message of hope. When I look at where we are relative to when I started my career some 32 years ago I am filled with hope. Why?

Energy generation and de-carbonization

Well, first up we are making astonishing gains in energy generation and de-carbonization. Removing our reliance on fossil fuels is a key element in improving the sustainability of our energy supply and becoming a more regenerative economy. This is happening, and fast.

The carbon intensity of a kWh of electricity refers to the amount of carbon dioxide (CO_2) emitted per unit of electricity generated, typically measured in grams of CO_2 per kWh. The carbon intensity of electricity varies by country and over time due to differences in energy sources and generation technologies.

According to data from the International Energy Agency, the global average carbon intensity of electricity has decreased from 570 grams of CO_2 per kWh in 2000 to 475 grams of CO_2 per kWh in 2020, representing a reduction of 17 per cent. While this doesn't seem great (and it isn't) it hides significant geographic variations.

In the UK, the carbon intensity of electricity has decreased from 544 grams of CO_2 per kWh in 2000 to 184 grams of CO_2 per kWh in 2020, representing a reduction of 66 per cent. This reduction is really strong and is due to a shift away from coal-fired power plants and an increase in renewable energy sources, such as wind and solar. France, on the other hand, has a grid carbon intensity that sits at around 60 grams of CO_2. This is as a result of their huge investment in nuclear power, an energy source that brings with it many other environmental and societal problems.

In China, the carbon intensity of electricity has decreased from 1,161 grams of CO_2 per kWh in 2000 to 729 grams of CO_2 per kWh in 2020, representing a reduction of 37 per cent. This reduction is due to a shift away from coal-fired power plants and is expected to accelerate, and

China now dominates the manufacture of many global renewable technologies.

In the United States, the carbon intensity of electricity has decreased from 633 grams of CO_2 per kWh in 2000 to 437 grams of CO_2 per kWh in 2020, representing a reduction of 31 per cent. This reduction is due to a shift away from coal-fired power plants and an increase in natural gas, which emits less CO_2 than coal, as well as an increase in renewable energy sources, such as wind and solar. The United States has a love affair with fracking (the gasification of coal measures) that continues to stunt and hinder their investment in renewables. There are significant policy challenges around fossil fuels that are unique to the United States.

It's worth noting that these figures are averages and that there may be significant regional variations within each country, as well as differences in the way the carbon intensity of electricity is calculated.

Regenerative agriculture

Second is the interest in regenerative agriculture as a practical way of:

- offsetting carbon
- ensuring future harvests
- reducing flood risk
- increasing the nutritional benefit of food
- increasing biodiversity
- improving water quality
- increasing agricultural profitability
- creating jobs

Regenerative agricultural is a revolutionary approach to food and sustainability (and all of the above) that comes from the past to show us the future. All cultures practiced an approach aligned with regenerative agriculture at one point because it was the only way of guaranteeing next year, literally. Over time it has become less prevalent as the chemical industry produced pesticides, fertilizers, herbicides and ultimately genetically modified seeds that increased profitability under the cloak of 'we need to feed the world' while ultimately reducing our ability to do just that. This is a truly exciting revolution and it's important for consumers to get behind it and put pressure on brands and retailers to adopt these principles. Regenerative agriculture fills me with hope.

Environmental entrepreneurship

Every business accelerator I've looked at now has a sustainability module built in. Environmental entrepreneurship has gone mainstream and this is supported by the myriad of data that shows that businesses with a clear and well-defined purpose do better in terms of financial performance and talent attraction than those businesses without a clear purpose. I lecture at universities across the UK and the vast majority of university courses have an environmental element to each course. We are increasingly seeing sustainability as part of every course. The reality is that sustainability skills are totally transferrable and incredibly desirable. This aligns with the big business opportunities of the next 10 years. This clearly includes AI (more on that in a moment) but also sustainability. Nearly every analysis of opportunities and trends includes sustainability.

The carbon removals market

This is set to boom and mature with predictions of $220 per tonne for quality carbon removals by 2030. Read that again: $220 a tonne. This is astonishing as it will create a rush of investment into projects that sequester carbon. There's money to be made here.

Net gain

It's really easy to criticize net gain as a concept. But it is increasingly being built into the planning world (in the UK all developments granted planning permission will need to demonstrate 10 per cent biodiversity net gain after November 2023). This is complex, for example how the heck do you measure it? Who polices it and what is their expertise? But I don't want to dwell on these issues, we will find a way. I just dig the fact that everyone applying for planning permission will need to at least have the conversation about net gain. Game changing in my opinion.

It is really easy to be overwhelmed by the enormity of the challenges that we face. It is only natural. But slowly, surely, we are all taking action – whether we plan to be or not we are part of a movement.

Business is at the forefront of this movement as nearly everything we do, buy, own or touch is made by people who work together in a company. The very word company is about community. It is formed of two words: Com, from the Latin for together, and Pan, from Panis meaning bread or to feed. Forming a company is simply breaking bread together. It is about companionship (literally) and creativity, about growing good as well as making a profit. Oikos – ecology and economy. Bedfellows rather than enemies.

Notes

Introduction

1 S Ze Yu. Why substantial Chinese FDI is flowing into Africa. Africa@ LSE, 2 April 2021. https://blogs.lse.ac.uk/africaatlse/2021/04/02/ why-substantial-chinese-fdi-is-flowing-into-africa-foreign-direct-investment/ (archived at https://perma.cc/Q354-CGD4)

Chapter 1: Where are we and how did we get here?

1 K Pierre-Louis. How to buy clothes that are built to last. *The New York Times*, 25 September 2019. www.nytimes.com/interactive/2019/climate/ sustainable-clothing.html (archived at https://perma.cc/XKB2-YUR7)

Chapter 2: You can't make money from a dead planet

1 BBC. Apple fined for slowing down old iPhones. *BBC News*, 7 February 2020. www.bbc.co.uk/news/technology-51413724 (archived at https:// perma.cc/X9SY-W7QF)

2 NCEI (n.d.) Climate monitoring. www.ncei.noaa.gov/monitoring (archived at https://perma.cc/Q6TN-AV4V)

Chapter 3: The main environmental challenges

1   NASA (n.d.) How long have sea levels been rising? How does recent sea-level rise compare to that over the previous centuries? NASA Sea Level Change. https://sealevel.nasa.gov/faq/13/how-long-have-sea-levels-been-rising-how-does-recent-sea-level-rise-compare-to-that-over-the-previous/ (archived at https://perma.cc/2GPA-E4SL)

2   IPBES. Global assessment report on biodiversity and ecosystem services, 2019. www.ipbes.net/global-assessment-report-biodiversity-ecosystem-services (archived at https://perma.cc/UW8L-96WT)

3   IPBES. 2020 living planet report, 2020. www.ipbes.net/global-assessment-report-biodiversity-ecosystem-services (archived at https://perma.cc/AN4B-M62D)

4   IPBES. Global assessment report on biodiversity and ecosystem services, 2019. www.ipbes.net/global-assessment-report-biodiversity-ecosystem-services (archived at https://perma.cc/UW8L-96WT)

5   WWF. Living Planet Report 2018. www.worldwildlife.org/pages/living-planet-report-2018 (archived at https://perma.cc/U7LC-6VA6)

6   C A Hallmann et al. More than 75 per cent decline over 27 years in total flying insect biomass in protected areas. PLoS ONE 12 (10), 2017. https://doi.org/10.1371/journal.pone.0185809 (archived at https://perma.cc/X54N-TZG6)

7   NOAA. Ocean acidification: A wake-up call in our waters. NOAA, 1 April 2016. www.noaa.gov/ocean-acidification-high-co2-world-dangerous-waters-ahead (archived at https://perma.cc/6PN9-PY8T)

Chapter 4: Business impacts

1   WWF. Hidden waste report 2020, 2020. www.noaa.gov/ocean-acidification-high-co2-world-dangerous-waters-ahead (archived at https://perma.cc/8GEG-NXYL)

2   R Smithers. Almost half of the world's food thrown away, report finds. *The Guardian*, 10 January 2013. www.theguardian.com/environment/2013/ jan/10/half-world-food-waste (archived at https://perma.cc/JP64-NF82)

3   International Solid Waste Association. A roadmap for closing waste dumpsites: The world's most polluted places, 2016. https://ars.org.ar/news/ ISWA_Roadmap_Report.pdf (archived at https://perma.cc/876E-YB3L)

4   UK Parliament. MPs call for ban on all plastic waste exports. UK Parliament, 7 November 2022. https://committees.parliament.uk/ committee/52/environment-food-and-rural-affairs-committee/news/ 174191/mps-call-for-ban-on-all-plastic-waste-exports/#:~:text= The%20UK%20exports%20around%2060,environmental%20and% 20human%20health%20impacts (archived at https://perma.cc/ X2K3-R2FB)

5   Alzheimer's Research UK. Air pollution and dementia risk review suggests particulate matter has greatest effect. Alzheimer's Research UK News, 26 October 2022. www.alzheimersresearchuk.org/air-pollution- and-dementia-risk-review-suggests-particulate-matter-has-greatest-effect/ (archived at https://perma.cc/ABQ7-EKTW)

6   Parkinson's Foundation. PD & pollution: Something in the air. Parkinson's Today Blog, 22 August 2022. www.parkinson.org/blog/ science-news/air-pollution (archived at https://perma.cc/TTF8-899V)

7   Gov.uk. Public health outcomes framework, 2023. https://fingertips.phe. org.uk/profile/public-health-outcomes-framework/data#page/4/ gid/1000043/pat/159/par/K02000001/ati/15/are/E92000001/iid/93861/ age/230/sex/4/cat/-1/ctp/-1/yrr/1/cid/4/tbm/1 (archived at https://perma. cc/47XJ-M5LH)

8   H Ritchie. How have the world's energy sources changed over the last two centuries? Our World in Data, 1 December 2021. https:// ourworldindata.org/global-energy-200-years (archived at https://perma. cc/WKW9-WGGQ)

9   OECD. OECD environmental outlook to 2050: The consequences of inaction – key facts and figures, 2012. www.oecd.org/env/indicators- modelling-outlooks/oecdenvironmentaloutlookto2050theconsequenceso finaction-keyfactsandfigures.htm (archived at https://perma.cc/6V6U- CKTP)

10   M Michot Foss and J Koelsch. 2022. Of Chinese Behemoths: What China's Rare Earths Dominance Means for the US. Research paper no. 12.19.22. Rice University's Baker Institute for Public Policy, Houston, Texas. https://doi.org/10.25613/5ZTC-WP59 (archived at https://perma.cc/37GU-PGAU)

11   J Bai, X Xu, Y Duan, G Zhang, Z Wang, L Wang and C Zheng. Evaluation of resource and environmental carrying capacity in rare earth mining areas in China, *Scientific Reports*, 2022, 12 (1), 6105

Chapter 5: Is there any good news?

1   IPSOS. Climate change: A growing skepticism. IPSOS News, 8 December 2022. www.ipsos.com/en/obscop-2022 (archived at https://perma.cc/T8FU-GT6U)

2   M Rao and R A Powell. The climate crisis and the rise of eco-anxiety. BMJ Opinion, 6 October 2021. https://blogs.bmj.com/bmj/2021/10/06/the-climate-crisis-and-the-rise-of-eco-anxiety/ (archived at https://perma.cc/E4VE-U24Q)

3   E Marks, C Hickman, C Panu, et al. Young people's voices on climate anxiety, government betrayal and moral injury: A global phenomenon, *Lancet Preprints*, 2021. http://dx.doi.org/10.2139/ssrn.3918955 (archived at https://perma.cc/4WW4-4PAZ)

4   W Mathis. Renewable returns tripled versus fossil fuels in last decade. *Bloomberg*, 18 March 2021. www.bloomberg.com/news/articles/2021-03-18/renewable-returns-tripled-versus-fossil-fuels-in-last-decade?leadSource=uverify%20wall (archived at https://perma.cc/95L4-ZKXS)

5   IEA (n.d.) Energy subsidies: Tracking the impact of fossil-fuel subsidies. www.iea.org/topics/energy-subsidies (archived at https://perma.cc/4MZD-L93G)

6   IEA. How much will renewable energy benefit from global stimulus packages? Fuel Report, 1 December 2021. www.iea.org/articles/how-much-will-renewable-energy-benefit-from-global-stimulus-packages (archived at https://perma.cc/W533-F493)

7   V Masterson. This map reveals clean energy jobs now outnumber
    fossil-fuel ones. World Economic Forum, 22 September 2022. www.
    weforum.org/agenda/2022/09/iea-clean-energy-jobs/ (archived at
    https://perma.cc/U4AU-ST3Q)

8   M Liebreich. Liebreich: The next half-trillion-dollar market –
    electrification of heat. BloombergNEF, 26 April 2023. https://about.
    bnef.com/blog/liebreich-the-next-half-trillion-dollar-market-
    electrification-of-heat/ (archived at https://perma.cc/S4XQ-ZQXQ)

9   IRENA. Renewable energy statistics 2022, 2022. www.irena.org/
    publications/2022/Jul/Renewable-Energy-Statistics-2022 (archived at
    https://perma.cc/KZX3-ZBNQ)

10 IEA. Hydropower special market report: Executive summary. IEA, June
    2021. www.iea.org/reports/hydropower-special-market-report/
    executive-summary (archived at https://perma.cc/NH9N-7FRK)

11 CarbonBrief (n.d.) How the UK transformed its electricity supply in
    just a decade. https://interactive.carbonbrief.org/how-uk-transformed-
    electricity-supply-decade/ (archived at https://perma.cc/SFT4-C229)

12 A Gray. Around 90% of all river-borne plastic that ends up in the
    ocean comes from just 10 rivers. World Economic Forum, 8 June 2018.
    www.weforum.org/agenda/2018/06/90-of-plastic-polluting-our-oceans-
    comes-from-just-10-rivers/ (archived at https://perma.cc/8MQY-WKR7)

13 European Commission (n.d.) Road transport: Reducing CO_2 emissions
    from vehicles. https://climate.ec.europa.eu/eu-action/transport-emissions/
    road-transport-reducing-co2-emissions-vehicles_en#:~:text=CO%E2%
    82%82%20emission%20performance%20standards%20for,EU%20
    emissions%20of%20carbon (archived at https://perma.cc/WPM6-MJ8G)

14 EPA. Carbon pollution from transportation, 2023. www.epa.gov/
    transportation-air-pollution-and-climate-change/carbon-pollution-
    transportation#:~:text=%E2%80%8BGreenhouse%20gas%20
    (GHG)%20emissions,contributor%20of%20U.S.%20GHG%20
    emissions (archived at https://perma.cc/9N88-G4T9)

15 BloombergNEF. What's new in EVO 2022? https://bnef.turtl.co/story/
    evo-2022/page/2/1?teaser=yes (archived at https://perma.cc/6UK4-H7JX)

16   Policy Department for Structural and Cohesion Policies. Environmental challenges through the life cycle of battery electric vehicles. TRAN Committee, March 2023. www.europarl.europa.eu/RegData/etudes/STUD/2023/733112/IPOL_STU(2023)733112_EN.pdf (archived at https://perma.cc/8V49-8UVB)

17   L La Picirelli de Souza, E E Silva Lora, J C Escobar Palacio, M H Rocha, M L Grillo Renó and O J Venturini. Comparative environmental life cycle assessment of conventional vehicles with different fuel options, plug-in hybrid and electric vehicles for a sustainable transportation system in Brazil, *Journal of Cleaner Production*, 2018, 203, 444–68. https://doi.org/10.1016/j.jclepro.2018.08.236 (archived at https://perma.cc/U8XU-E52V)

18   G Bieker. A global comparison of the life-cycle greenhouse gas emissions of combustion engine and electric passenger cars. The ICCT, 20 July 2021. https://theicct.org/publication/a-global-comparison-of-the-life-cycle-greenhouse-gas-emissions-of-combustion-engine-and-electric-passenger-cars/ (archived at https://perma.cc/SE8Q-NMDV)

19   IEA. The role of critical minerals in clean energy transitions. IEA, May 2021. www.iea.org/reports/the-role-of-critical-minerals-in-clean-energy-transitions (archived at https://perma.cc/CMP9-8USJ)

20   X Xia and P Li. A review of the life cycle assessment of electric vehicles: Considering the influence of batteries, *Science of The Total Environment*, 2022, 814, 152870. www.sciencedirect.com/science/article/abs/pii/S0048969721079493 (archived at https://perma.cc/FJS6-QJXS)

21   J Montoya-Torres, O Akizu-Gardoki and M Iturrondobeitia. Measuring life-cycle carbon emissions of private transportation in urban and rural settings, *Sustainable Cities and Society*, 2023, 96, 104658. www.sciencedirect.com/science/article/pii/S221067072300269X (archived at https://perma.cc/5YJF-Y4B2)

22   BloombergNEF. Electric vehicle outlook 2022, 2021. https://bnef.turtl.co/story/evo-2022/page/1?teaser=yes (archived at https://perma.cc/ZF73-2TLV)

23   IEA. The role of critical minerals in clean energy transitions. IEA, May 2021. www.iea.org/reports/the-role-of-critical-minerals-in-clean-energy-transitions (archived at https://perma.cc/SSD2-2C8R)

24   M Gilleran, E Bonnema and J Woods. Impact of electric vehicle charging on the power demand of retail buildings, *Advances in Applied Energy*, 2021, 4, 100062. www.nrel.gov/docs/fy21osti/79080.pdf (archived at https://perma.cc/8CAY-BA8E)

25   D Nichols. The future of EV batteries. GreenCars, May 2023. www.greencars.com/greencars-101/the-future-of-ev-batteries (archived at https://perma.cc/KEA4-BP4U)

26   UT News. New cobalt-free lithium-ion battery reduces costs without sacrificing performance. UT News, 14 July 2020. https://news.utexas.edu/2020/07/14/new-cobalt-free-lithium-ion-battery-reduces-costs-without-sacrificing-performance/ (archived at https://perma.cc/ZVY2-REC4)

27   C Elton. 'Significant breakthrough': This new sea salt battery has 4 times the capacity of lithium. *EuroNews*, 14 December 2022. www.euronews.com/green/2022/12/13/significant-breakthrough-this-new-sea-salt-battery-has-4-times-the-capacity-of-lithium (archived at https://perma.cc/FT8V-DHE3)

28   Global Cement and Concrete Association. Global cement and concrete industry announces roadmap to achieve groundbreaking 'net zero' CO_2 emissions by 2050. GCCA, 12 October 2021. https://gccassociation.org/news/global-cement-and-concrete-industry-announces-roadmap-to-achieve-groundbreaking-net-zero-co2-emissions-by-2050/ (archived at https://perma.cc/84K2-SCE2)

29   M Nieuwenhuis, C Knight, T Postmes and S A Haslam. The relative benefits of green versus lean office space: Three field experiments, *Journal of Experimental Psychology Applied*, 2014, 20 (3). www.researchgate.net/publication/264395358_The_Relative_Benefits_of_Green_Versus_Lean_Office_Space_Three_Field_Experiments (archived at https://perma.cc/62WR-DCZD)

30   Business Wire. Navigant research report shows global revenue for commercial building automation solutions is anticipated to exceed \$44B by 2029. *Business Wire*, 25 March 2020. www.businesswire.com/news/home/20200325005467/en/Navigant-Research-Report-Shows-Global-Revenue-for-Commercial-Building-Automation-Solutions-Is-Anticipated-to-Exceed-44B-by-2029 (archived at https://perma.cc/6E9A-2M8S)

31 C Arsenault. Only 60 years of farming left if soil degradation
continues. *Scientific American*, 5 December 2014. www.
scientificamerican.com/article/only-60-years-of-farming-left-if-soil-
degradation-continues/ (archived at https://perma.cc/XD93-DD6D)

32 Food Insight. Consumer perspectives on regenerative agriculture. *Food
Insight*, 10 February 2022. https://foodinsight.org/consumer-
perspectives-on-regenerative-agriculture/ (archived at https://perma.cc/
X65E-ZK5J)

33 BBMG. Radically better food. BBMG, 4 June 2021. https://bbmg.com/
radically-better-food/ (archived at https://perma.cc/8V35-BSYD)

34 Reuters Staff. Celebrities back call for climate action in Extinction
Rebellion video. *Reuters*, 3 November 2019. www.reuters.com/article/
us-climate-change-protests-celebrities-idUSKBN1XD06C (archived at
https://perma.cc/94EM-EWPK)

35 T Clark, S Pickering and A Rizvi (2020) *Global Landscape of Public
Retirement System Investment in Fossil Fuels.* Institute for Energy
Economics and Financial Analysis (IEEFA), Lakewood, OH

Chapter 6: How do we do good and still turn a profit?

1 McKinsey & Company. Consumers care about sustainability – and back
it up with their wallets. McKinsey, 6 February 2023. www.mckinsey.
com/industries/consumer-packaged-goods/our-insights/consumers-care-
about-sustainability-and-back-it-up-with-their-wallets (archived at
https://perma.cc/S2NB-5HJC)

2 eunomia. How circular is glass? September 2022. https://cdn.ca.emap.
com/wp-content/uploads/sites/6/2022/09/ZWE-glass-report-summary.
pdf (archived at https://perma.cc/HCF2-KQU8)

3 RECOUP. UK household plastics collection survey 2022, 2022. www.
recoup.org/p/444/uk-household-plastic-packaging-collection-survey-
2022 (archived at https://perma.cc/R7DN-Z8TZ)

4   Packaging Europe. Recycling rates for aluminium cans almost 73% in various EU countries, according to new report. *Packaging Europe News*, 16 December 2022. https://packagingeurope.com/news/recycling-rates-for-aluminium-cans-almost-73-in-various-eu-countries-according-to-new-report/9207.article (archived at https://perma.cc/8AYG-MG8N)

5   J Chu. Footwear's (carbon) footprint. *MIT News*, 22 May 2013. https://news.mit.edu/2013/footwear-carbon-footprint-0522#:~:text=A%20typical%20pair%20of%20running,new%20MIT%2Dled%20lifecycle%20assessment (archived at https://perma.cc/BZJ6-RBA7)

6   E Farra. Should fashion be labelled by its carbon footprint, similar to the calories listed on our food? *British Vogue*, 15 April 2020. www.vogue.co.uk/fashion/article/allbirds-sneakers-labeled-by-carbon-footprint (archived at https://perma.cc/FN8W-73ZN)

7   L Siedel, M Ketzer, E Broman, et al. Weakened resilience of benthic microbial communities in the face of climate change, *ISME Communications*, 2022, 2, 21. www.nature.com/articles/s43705-022-00104-9 (archived at https://perma.cc/84PH-4B9R)

8   K Borgå, M A McKinney, H Routti, et al. The influence of global climate change on accumulation and toxicity of persistent organic pollutants and chemicals of emerging concern in Arctic food webs, *Environmental Science: Processes & Impacts*, 2022, 24, 1544–1576. https://pubs.rsc.org/en/content/articlehtml/2022/em/d1em00469g (archived at https://perma.cc/X9FB-9UNU)

9   S Fu. How cities can tackle both the affordable housing and climate crises. Housing Matters, 2 November 2022. https://housingmatters.urban.org/articles/how-cities-can-tackle-both-affordable-housing-and-climate-crises#:~ (archived at https://perma.cc/JK6H-54JK)

Chapter 7: The strategic tools you need to change your business

1   Business Wire. Recent study reveals more than a third of global consumers are willing to pay more for sustainability as demand grows for

environmentally-friendly alternatives. *Business Wire*, 14 October 2021. www.businesswire.com/news/home/20211014005090/en/Recent-Study-Reveals-More-Than-a-Third-of-Global-Consumers-Are-Willing-to-Pay-More-for-Sustainability-as-Demand-Grows-for-Environmentally-Friendly-Alternatives (archived at https://perma.cc/2CCJ-SH5Z)

2   PwC. February 2023 global consumer insights pulse survey. PwC, 16 February 2023. www.pwc.com/consumerinsights (archived at https://perma.cc/GU9D-LECR)

3   R Edelman. The belief-driven employee. Edelman, 31 August 2021. www.edelman.com/trust/2021-trust-barometer/belief-driven-employee/new-employee-employer-compact (archived at https://perma.cc/ZU5Z-TT8J)

Chapter 8: The practical and science-based tools to change your business (and still make a profit)

1   Grand View Research. Graphene market size, share & trends analysis report by product (graphene oxide, graphene nanoplatelets), by application (electronics, composites, energy), by region, and segment forecasts, 2023–2030. GVR, 2021. www.grandviewresearch.com/industry-analysis/graphene-industry#:~:text=The%20global%20graphene%20market%20size%20was%20estimated%20at%20USD%20175.9,USD%203%2C752.9%20million%20by%202030 (archived at https://perma.cc/3U6E-TKW5)

2   MIT. Soil-based carbon sequestration. MIT Climate Portal, 15 April 2021. https://climate.mit.edu/explainers/soil-based-carbon-sequestration (archived at https://perma.cc/W3UP-UYKB)

3   D J Beerling, E P Kantzas, M R Lomas, et al. Potential for large-scale CO_2 removal via enhanced rock weathering with croplands, *Nature*, 2020, 583, 242–48

Chapter 9: Re-framing business

1 Paris Collaborative on Green Budgeting. Climate change and long term fiscal sustainability. OECD, 16–17 March 2020. www.oecd.org/gov/budgeting/scoping-paper-on-fiscal-sustainability-and-climate-change.pdf (archived at https://perma.cc/KWB3-ECW3)

2 H Hoikkala. H&M boss warns of 'terrible social consequences' if people ditch fast fashion. *Independent*, 28 October 2019. www.independent.co.uk/news/business/news/hm-fast-fashion-boss-karl-johan-persson-environmental-damage-a9174121.html (archived at https://perma.cc/T4T9-WFVY)

'The last chapter'

1 J D Nobles, D Radley, O T Mytton and Whole Systems Obesity programme team. The Action Scales Model: A conceptual tool to identify key points for action within complex adaptive systems, 2022, 142 (6), 328–37. https://pubmed.ncbi.nlm.nih.gov/33998333/ (archived at https://perma.cc/66Q5-KCXP)

Index

A Plastic Ocean 98
Action Scales Model 258–60
Adidas 120–21
advanced weathering for
    sequestration 203–05
advertising, making environmental
    claims 194–99
Africa, Chinese investment in 9
Allbirds 120–21
aluminium packaging 117–20
An Inconvenient Truth 98
Apple 15–16
Arrhenius, Svante 20
artisan jeans 42–43, 241
automotive industry, decline of the
    ICE and rise of EVs 77–83

B-Corps 109
Barry, Mike 89
battery electric vehicles (BEVs)
    see electric vehicles (EVs)
battery technology, developments
    in 81–82
Ben & Jerry's 102–03
biodiversity, benefits of regenerative
    agriculture 86
biodiversity loss
    increasing rate of 25–28
    major reasons for 26–27
biological recovery cycle 38–41
biological sequestration of
    carbon 202–03
blended consumption 95–96
Blue Planet (BBC) 112
Boers, Niklas 31
brand authenticity 99–103
brand management 106–07
brand personality 129–31
Brexit 156, 251
Brondízio, Eduardo S 26

Brother 100
Budweiser 102
building automation systems
    (BAS) 84
built environment, sustainable
    building design 83–84
business
    companies' loss of purpose 15
    influence of environmental
        activism 96–99
    need for critical and creative
        thinking 89–90
    role in solving environmental
        problems 211, 267
    staying relevant to
        consumers 110
    survival in a changing
        world 256–57
business culture
    building a good culture 149–51
    definition of 148–49
    embedding sustainability
        in 148–54
    measuring and managing
        sustainability 151–54
business impacts 37–67
    energy 37, 55–59
    resource use 37, 60–67
    waste 37, 38–54
business models
    risk-averse nature of 216–17
    risk of short-term
        planning 214–17
    transition to regenerative
        business 231–32, 240–41
business success, measures
    of 210–11
business transformation 104–25
    changing approaches to
        sustainability 105–10

business transformation (*Continued*)
    checklist for building a better
      business 207–09
    consumers' understanding of the
      science 111–21
    determining environmental
      impact 121–25
    extending the scope of your
      environmental policy
      137–40
    how to begin thinking about
      sustainability 128–29
    how to write an environmental
      policy 131–36
    how to write an environmental
      strategy 140–54
    meaning of 'better'
      business 104–10
    start with a clear purpose
      129–31
    strategic tools for change
      126–54
    understanding your
      environmental impacts
      155–209
    where to focus attention on
      environmental impact
      121–25
    Why Statement 129–31
    see also regenerative business
Business Transformation
    Compass 223–25

Callendar, Guy 20
capitalism
    approach to making
      money 249–51
    consequences of 7–10
    need for reform 17–18
    need for systems change 257
carbon capture and storage 202
carbon cycle 21–22
carbon dioxide (CO_2)

    energy-related emissions
      projections 59
    greenhouse gas 22
    levels in the atmosphere 20–21
carbon emissions
    global impact of Covid-19
      lockdowns 252, 254–55
    reduction in energy-related
      emissions 74
    setting science-based reduction
      targets 199–201
carbon footprint *see* carbon impact
    assessment
carbon impact assessment (carbon
    footprint) 155–70
    carbon as a metric 156–57
    definition and purpose of 157
    Greenhouse Gas (GHG)
      Protocol 158
    how to undertake a Scope 1 and
      Scope 2 audit 156–70
    methodology 157–70
    Scope 1 GHG emissions 158,
      159–61
    Scope 2 GHG emissions 159,
      161–62
    Scope 3 GHG emissions 159,
      163–70
    ways to determine
      environmental impact
      121–25
carbon literacy training 206
carbon nanotube electrodes 82
carbon offsetting schemes 205
carbon removals market 267
carbon sequestration 201–05
Carson, Rachel 27–28
carton-board back packaging
    113–14, 117–20
CFCs (chlorofluorocarbons)
    23–24
    impact on the ozone layer
      34–36

change
  future of business 256–57
  re-framing business 210–19
  systems change models 258–61
change points, opportunities for
  creativity 217–19
Chasing Ice 98
China, investment in Africa 9
circular economy 120
  cycles of 38–44
  design models 41–44
  plastic 75–76
clean-up efforts, plastic
  pollution 76–77
climate anxiety 68–69
climate change 19–24
  carbon cycle 21–22
  consequences of short-term
    policy thinking 212–17
  creating resilient
    ecosystems 87–88
  discretionary impact
    through policy measure
    spending 214–17
  factors influencing global
    warming 22–24
  greenhouse effect 22–24
  greenhouse gases 22–24
  impacts of rising CO_2 levels
    20–21
  non-discretionary impacts on
    public spending 213
  range of impacts 20
climate scepticism 69
CO_2 *see* carbon dioxide
coal *see* energy
cobalt
  demand for 81
  environmental impacts of
    mining 66–67
cobalt-free batteries 82
colonialism 9, 257

communications, transition to
  regenerative business
  236–37, 244–45
community health, benefits of
  regenerative agriculture 87
competitive advantage 109–10
consumerism
  drivers of mass consumption 12
  emergence of 12
  promotion of 10
consumers
  aspirations 92, 93–94
  changes in their behaviours 92,
    94–96
  demand for food with less
    environmental impact 87–88
  environmental education 88–90
  macro beliefs 91, 92
  micro beliefs 91, 92–93
  trends in decision making
    126–28
  understanding of the
    science 111–21
  understanding their changing
    beliefs 90–96
  understanding their
    environmental
    concerns 143, 144
  value–action gap 94–95
  waste produced by 44
corporate social responsibility
  policy 137
Covid-19 lockdowns, impact on
  global emissions 252,
  254–55
Cowspiracy 98
creativity 211–19
  definition of 211–12
  exploiting the opportunity in
    crisis 217–19
  imagining a different
    world 211–19

de-carbonization, positive
        developments 263–65
Dell 130
demand, designing into
        products 16–18
design
    product design with less
        environmental impact
        171–85
    transition to regenerative
        business 233–34, 242–43
Díaz, Sandra 25–26
documentaries about environmental
        issues 98–99
Double Diamond process 241, 261
Dove 102
drinks packaging (example),
        environmental impact of
        different materials 112–20
Drucker, Peter 239
Dyson 44

Earth Overshoot Day 60
eco anxiety 68
economic justice 228–29
economy
    benefits of regenerative
        agriculture 86–87
    link with ecology 11–12
electric vehicles (EVs)
    business case for 77–78, 82–83
    developments in battery
        technology 81–82
    rise of 77–83
electricity, growth of renewable
        sources 70–74
emotional obsolescence 16–18
energy 37
    demand projections 59
    electricity production 57,
        263–65
    global energy consumption over
        time 55–56

global energy reserves 58–59
    positive developments 70–74,
        263–65
environment, social, governance
        (ESG) approach 138–40
environmental activism
    documentaries about
        environmental issues 98–99
    rise of 96–98
environmental audit 155
        see also carbon impact
        assessment (carbon
        footprint)
environmental challenges 19–36
    biodiversity loss 25–28
    climate change 19–24
    ocean health 28–33
    ozone depletion 34–36
environmental claims, how to talk
        about 194–99
environmental crisis, separation
        of science, art and
        humanities 6–7
environmental education
        88–90
environmental entrepreneurship,
        positive developments 266
environmental impact
    calculations 42–44
    drinks packaging (example)
        112–20
    including in your environmental
        strategy 142–43
    lower impact manufacturing
        processes 185–94
    product design with less
        impact 170–85
    trainers/sneakers
        (example) 120–21
    use of carbon as a metric
        121–25
    ways to determine 121–25
environmental justice 225–26

environmental policy
corporate social responsibility
policy 137
environment, social, governance
(ESG) approach 138–40
extending the scope of 137–40
how to write a policy
document 131–36
policy refinement 143–44
sustainable development
policy 137–38
environmental strategy
action 141
canvas for 147–48
change mission 141
checklist for building a better
business 207–09
embed sustainability in business
culture 148–54
environmental impacts 142–43
how to write a strategy
document 140–54
identify ideas and
opportunities 145–48
policy refinement 143–44
sustainability vision 140–42
training your team 206
understanding your
environmental impacts
155–209
values 140–41
what your customers care
about 143, 144
experts, distrust of 156
Extinction Rebellion (XR) 96–97

fashion industry
artisan denim 42–43, 241
designing demand into
products 17
fast fashion 8, 14–15, 17, 215–16
slow fashion 17
finance, transition to regenerative

business 238–39, 245–49
fishing industry, impacts on ocean
health 32
food industry, wasted food 44–47
food production, regenerative
agriculture 85–88
forests and woodlands, as carbon
sinks 202
Forum for the Future model 223–25
fossil fuel industry
level of investment in 97–98
subsidizing of 71–72
fossil fuels, rise in use of 55
functional obsolescence 13–15

Gamechangers 98
General Motors 78
geological sequestration
of carbon 202
geothermal energy 73
glass as a packaging material 115,
117–20
global warming potential
(GWP) 23, 46
graphene 202
The Great Recovery 41–42
greencocking 194–96
greenhouse effect 22–24
Greenhouse Gas (GHG)
Protocol 158
greenhouse gases 22–24
landfill site emissions 48–49
waste incinerator emissions
51–54
green-hushing 196–97
greenwashing 108–09, 194
Guide to Critical Shifts 224
Gulf Stream
functions of 28–29
impacts of disruption 31

H&M 216
Halo 120

human population projections
60–61
human resources (HR), transition to
regenerative business
237–38, 245
hydro power 74
hydrogen fuel cells 78

iFixit Repairability Index 16
imagining a different world 211–19
incineration of waste 51–54
industrial revolution 55
Innovate UK 251
innovation
role of sustainability 11
transition to regenerative
business 232–33, 241–42
Insulate Britain 97
internal combustion engine (ICE),
decline of 77–83

Kaepernick, Colin 100–01
Kennedy, John F 217, 218
key performance indicators
(KPIs) 151

labour, exploitation of 7–10
Labour movement 8
landfill disposal of waste 47–49
leadership, transition to
regenerative business
230–31, 240
lean manufacturing, waste
minimization 186–94
leased products 43–44
Liebreich, Michael 72
light bulb industry, Phoebus
cartel 14
lithium, demand for 81–82
Loop 120
low-wage manufacturing
centres 8–10

Ma, Jack 61
manganese, demand for 81
manufacturing, lower impact
manufacturing
processes 185–94
marketing, transition to
regenerative business
236–37, 244–45
Marks & Spencer Plan A
programme 89, 151
Marx, Karl 7
Mazzucato, Mariana 249–50
meditation, aid to creative
thinking 146–47
methane (CH_4)
global warming potential
(GWP) 46
greenhouse gas 23
Microsoft 16
Midgley, Thomas, Jnr 34
Monbiot, George 32
Montreal Protocol (1987) 34–36
Mud Jeans 241
Musk, Elon 61

natural cycle see biological recovery
cycle
natural gas see energy
net gain 267
net zero, setting science-based
targets 199–201
Next 14–15
nickel, demand for 81
Nike 100–01, 120–21
nitrogen oxides (NOx) 51, 52, 53
nitrous oxide (N_2O), greenhouse
gas 23
non-expert influencers 156–57

obsolescence, planned 13–18
The Ocean Cleanup 77
ocean health 28–33

acidification 30–31, 203
Blue Planet (BBC) 112
functions of the ocean
    currents 28–29, 31
impacts of rising
    temperatures 29–31
impacts of the fishing
    industry 32
plastic pollution 32–33
potential disruption of the Gulf
    Stream 31
sources of pollution 32–33
warming effects 24
oceans, carbon storage in 203
oil *see* energy
On Running 120
operations, transition to
    regenerative business
    234–35, 243–44
ozone (O_3)
    greenhouse gas 23–24
    health problems associated
        with 51
ozone depletion, impact of
    CFCs 34–36

packaging, environmental impact of
    different materials 112–20
Packard, Vance 12–13
Paris Agreement (2015) 58, 199
Parley 120
Patagonia 101–02
Persson, Karl-Johan 216
PET (polyethylene terephthalate)
    packaging 115–16, 117
Phoebus cartel (light bulb
    industry) 14
planned obsolescence 13–18
plastic
    bans on single-use plastics 75
    Blue Planet (BBC) 112
    challenge of recycling different
        types 40–41
    disposal of waste 49–50

issues with biodegradable
    alternatives 76
pollution problem 32–33
positive developments 75–77
plastic bags, impacts of taxation
    on 76
PM2.5 particulate matter 51–52,
    53
Porritt, Jonathon 224
positive developments 69–103
    brand authenticity 99–103
    carbon removals market 267
    changing consumer beliefs and
        behaviour 90–96
    de-carbonization 263–65
    decline of the internal
        combustion engine 77–83
    documentaries about
        environmental issues
        98–99
    energy generation 263–65
    energy revolution 69–74
    environmental education 88–90
    environmental
        entrepreneurship 266
    net gain 267
    plastic pollution 75–77
    regenerative agriculture 85–88,
        265–66
    rise in environmental
        activism 96–98
    rise of electric vehicles
        (EVs) 77–83
    role of business in tackling
        challenges 267
    sustainable building design
        83–84
Potter, Clare 194
Producer Responsibility
    Obligations 108
product design *see* design
profit
    accumulation through
        exploitation 256–57

profit (*Continued*)
    approach to making
        money 249–51
    consequences of relentless
        pursuit of 7–10, 210–11
    future of business 256–57
    unsustainability of traditional
        approaches 11–12
profitability, building a better
    business 104–25
public sector entrepreneurship
    249–51

rare earth elements (REE) 62–67
rare earth oxides (REO) 62
raw materials, exploitation of 7–10
recycling, challenge of
        differentiating materials
        40–41
regenerative agriculture 85–88
    improved community health 87
    improved economic
        outcomes 86–87
    improved soil health 85–86
    increased biodiversity 86
    increased resilience to climate
        change 87–88
    positive developments 265–66
    reduced dependence on synthetic
        inputs 86
regenerative business 104, 220–55
    advantages and benefits
        of 221–22
    economic justice 228–29
    education and public awareness
        campaigns 222
    environmental justice 225–26
    forms of 220–21
    principles of 220
    social justice 227
    summary of actions
        needed 261–63
    transition challenges 222–25

Regenerative Business
    Navigator 229–55
    approach to making
        money 249–51
    business models 231–32,
        240–41
    communications/marketing
        236–37, 244–45
    design 233–34, 242–43
    finance 238–39, 245–49
    human resources (HR) 237–38,
        245
    innovation 232–33, 241–42
    leadership 230–31, 240
    operations 234–35, 243–44
    Regenerative Compass 260–61
    strategy 229–30, 239
    summary 252–55
Regenerative Compass 260–61
REI 102
renewable energy 70–74
    investment in 97
reputation management 106–07
resources
    demand for critical metals in EV
        manufacture 81–82
    overuse of 60
    ownership and control of 7–10,
        60–67
    scarcity of 61–67
    sustainability issues 65–67
    unsustainable use of 12
risk management 107–08

Salt, Titus 7–8
Samsung 16–17
science-based emissions reduction
    targets 199–201
science matters, consumer
    understanding of
    111–21
sea-water batteries 82
Seaspiracy 32, 98

sequestration of carbon 201–05
  carbon removals market 267
Settele, Josef 25–26
short-term policy thinking,
  consequences of 212–17
Silent Spring (Carson, 1962)
  27–28
Sinek, Simon 129–30
social justice 227
soil, as a carbon store 203
soil health, regenerative
  agriculture 85–86
solar power production 70–71
Standing Rock Sioux Tribe 96
Stop, Look and Listen
  approach 145–46
strategy
  tools for change 126–54
  transition to regenerative
    business 229–30, 239
sulphur dioxide (SOx) 51, 52, 53
suppliers
  role in brand authenticity 103
  supply-chain compliance 108
supply-chain compliance 108
sustainability
  changing approaches of
    business 105–10
  embedding in business
    culture 148–54
  environmental
    entrepreneurship 266
  how to begin thinking
    about 128–29
  Marks & Spencer Plan A
    programme 89, 151
  post-truth agenda 215
  role in innovation 11
sustainability vision 140–42
sustainable development
  policy 137–38
systems change, survival in a
  changing world 256–57
systems change models 258–61

technological obsolescence 15–16
technological recovery cycle 38, 39,
  41–44
Ted Talks, *Start with Why*
  (Sinek) 129–30
Tesla 77
Tetra packs (carton-board) 113–14,
  117–20
The Entrepreneurial State
  (Mazzucato, 2013) 249–50
The True Cost 98
The Waste Makers (Packard,
  1960) 12–13
Thomas, Sophie 42
Thompson, Hunter S 217
Thunberg, Greta 96
trainers/sneakers (example),
  environmental impact
  120–21
TV production as activism 98–99

unionization of workers 8

value–action gap in consumers
  94–95
values 140–41
Veja 120–21
Vienna Convention (1989) 34–36
volatile organic compounds
  (VOCs) 51, 53–54
Volkswagen 78

waste 37, 38–54
  biological recovery cycle 38–41
  consequences of mass
    consumption 12
  defining 38
  downstream impacts of 47–54
  exporting of 49–50
  food industry 44–47
  impacts of different disposal
    methods 47–54
  incineration (with energy
    recovery) 50–54

waste (*Continued*)
   landfill disposal 47–49
   planned obsolescence 13–18
   technological recovery cycle 38, 39, 41–44
waste hierarchy 47–48
waste minimization, lean manufacturing 189–94

water vapour (H_2O), greenhouse gas 22–24
Watt, James 55
weather, impacts of Gulf Stream disruption 31
wind power 72

Xerox 43–44